D1633994

THE YORKSHIRE POST: TWO CENTURIES

HER MAJESTY QUEEN ELIZABETH II

a Yorkshire Post *picture taken when, as Princess Elizabeth, she visited Harrogate in 1949. With the Princess is seen Ald. Thomas Tomlinson, chairman of the West Riding County Council.*

THE YORKSHIRE POST

POST

two centuries

BY

MILDRED A. GIBB, FRANK BECKWITH

and members of the Editorial Staff
of The Yorkshire Post and The Yorkshire Evening Post

Published by

The Yorkshire Conservative Newspaper Co. Ltd

1954

Made and printed in Great Britain

by Percy Lund, Humphries & Company Limited

Bradford and London

CONTENTS

ILLUSTRATIONS

INTRODUCTION

T. L. TAYLOR

Chairman of the Yorkshire Conservative Newspaper Company Limited

In the whole world very few newspapers have survived all the changes of two centuries. *The Yorkshire Post* has now attained that distinction, and my colleagues and I have felt that the achievement deserves to be permanently recorded. Readers of this book will learn how the traditions of the paper have been built up under the strain of crisis, challenge and response over the years.

The story begins a long way back in an England still mainly agricultural but standing expectant on the threshold of the Industrial Revolution. *The Leeds Intelligencer*, as the paper was entitled for 112 years, began only eight years after the defeat of Prince Charles Edward at Culloden. It became a well-written and energetic paper, recording and responding to the impulses and ambitions that revolutionized mechanical invention. The paper flourished through the years of swift scientific progress and of the astonishing development which followed its application to our industries, not least conspicuously in the West Riding.

The change into *The Yorkshire Post* in 1866 was a natural one. The supremacy of British trade had brought a ferment of ideas and ambitions to the region the paper served. A company was formed to expand the *Intelligencer* into a daily. A new name was chosen to indicate an appeal to a wider area; but there was no break with the long-established literary and political traditions. Sir Winston Churchill, who understands journalism so well, has written of what he calls transmogrifications when the goodwill of old papers is bought up and they abruptly appear as brand-new publications. The change of *The Leeds Intelligencer* into *The Yorkshire Post* made no break of that kind in continuity of thought and purpose. It seems to us entirely fitting to speak of our paper, despite its change of name on becoming a daily, as having lived for 200 years.

Faith in the new morning paper, like faith in the start of the *Intelligencer*, was justified by the circumstances of the time and the sound ideas of the proprietors. In that period of mid-Victorian expansion we had become the manufacturers and carriers of the world. Men wanted to study the best ways of developing our industrial world leadership. How a Conservative paper in the heart of a manufacturing region faced that unending series of problems is an instructive study. *The Yorkshire Post* helped to stimulate, and often led, no less faithfully than it recorded, the thinking of the North on crucial questions.

Through national triumph and national tragedy the paper has given faithful support to a Conservative philosophy, but never in the spirit of an unthinking partisan. It has thought out its own interpretation of the Party creed in new contexts. Sometimes, on important occasions, its view has differed from that of the Party leaders, as for example when it made its stand against appeasement of Hitler and Mussolini. But what was heresy to some when written usually became orthodox to almost all in the course of time. Though readers and sometimes many readers have disagreed with political doctrines *The Yorkshire Post* has defended, I think it is not too much to claim that they have recognized its use of the power of the Press for always worthy ends. They honour its long record of honesty and fairness.

The writing of this record of journalistic enterprise has involved much research. We are grateful to Miss Mildred A. Gibb (Mrs Arthur Dobson), the author of a number of historical works, who has helped to explore half-forgotten stages in the history of *The Yorkshire Post*, and to Mr Frank Beckwith, librarian of the Leeds Library, who, in tracing local history, has devoted patient study to the files of *The Leeds Intelligencer*. We are fortunate to have had the help of two such distinguished scholars. Their researches have been valuably supplemented by members of our staffs.

The authors of a history of this kind are bound to say much about directors, editors, and managers, but we never forget that the success and reputation of a paper are built up by the efforts of a much greater number of colleagues. We think of the reporters and sub-editors, often under the tyranny of the clock, as they strive to present a vivid, accurate account of the day's news. We admire the craftsmen who daily show their pride and skill in the mechanical processes of newspaper production. During the bleak Yorkshire winter we often think of the motor drivers delivering papers in fog and snow. These and many other loyal men and women make an indispensable contribution to our team.

Two centuries of struggle and achievement in the ever-changing world of politics and business: two centuries of development in news-gathering, printing, and advertising – this, we feel, is not only a proud record but also a story of deep interest to the general reader. Our theme is how successive generations, loyal to the principles of fairness and public service, built up the influence of a great newspaper.

J.R. Taylor

ACKNOWLEDGEMENT

We are indebted to Mr F. G. B. Hutchings, the Leeds City Librarian, always the friend of the seeker after enlightenment, for help at the Reference Library on many points of Leeds history that needed elucidation in the progress of this work.

CHAPTER I

A promising start and steady growth

[1754–1818]

Anyone who looks at the front page of *The Yorkshire Post* will note that alongside the number of the day's issue appears the statement 'established 1754'. The newspaper which was born 200 years ago in the days of King George II was named not *The Yorkshire Post* but *The Leeds Intelligencer*. This was first published on Tuesday, 2 July 1754, and survived under that title until Saturday, 30 June 1866. On the following Monday, 2 July, when it had completed 112 years of existence to the day, it became *The Yorkshire Post*. That is why this record of two centuries of newspaper enterprise in Leeds and the North of England is divided into two sections, one dealing with the history of *The Leeds Intelligencer* and the other with that of its successor. For some years after that July morning when the *Intelligencer* was transformed into the *Post* the title of the older journal was used as a sub-heading; but gradually the change of name was forgotten. Eventually the sub-title disappeared, and all that remained to bear witness to the tradition was the date 1754, still printed on each issue of the paper.

The Leeds Intelligencer was founded by Griffith Wright the elder, a vigorous, long-lived man, who was the son of the clerk of St John's Church, Briggate, Leeds. Whether he knew it or not at the time, he had chosen an extremely promising moment to launch his new venture. For these were days when Leeds was starting to emerge from its status as a busy market town for the woollen trade and to play a prominent part in the growth of industry that was to lead to the Industrial Revolution. As the towns of the busy North grew in importance, they began to contribute not only to the nation's wealth, but to its political discussion; and there was much to discuss. These were years of stimulating opportunity for journalists.

Force of public opinion made itself felt, slowly in the eighteenth century, but with gathering momentum early in the nineteenth, in spite of formidable odds against it. Governments resented challenges to their omnicompetence and placed barriers in the path of those who wished to arouse public discussion. The progress of the Leeds papers showed clearly that Yorkshire folk wanted news, first about what was happening across the seas, then about the intentions of their legislators at Westminster. At the start they got foreign news if they were prepared to wait for it and accept what the London papers had to offer; Parliamentary intelligence was not forthcoming without a fight; local news was scanty indeed in the early stages, consisting largely of paragraphs about curious natural phenomena and the eligibility of 'agreeable' maidens with handsome fortunes.

Not a great deal is known about Griffith Wright. He was born in 1732 or 1733 and married Mary Pullan in December 1755. After conducting his paper for thirty years, he handed it over to his son Thomas in June 1785 and saw him edit it for a further twenty years. He outlived Thomas, who died on 26 February 1805, by thirteen years, and during those years saw his grandson edit the paper. Thus, when he died on 27 October 1818, *The Leeds Intelligencer* could be called his life's work.

After his death the grandson quickly disposed of the business and retired like a typical Leeds worthy of the early nineteenth century. Griffith Wright junior had been born in 1784 and had succeeded to the business at an early age; he was able to relinquish it while still in his thirties, because latterly the profits of the paper, together with the ancillary trades of general printing and patent medicine selling, had been more than £1000 a year, a sum then worth at least six times what it is today. He progressed through the ranks of Common Councilman (1820) and Alderman (1833) to become the last Mayor of Leeds under the old Corporation (1834–5). He had a pretty wit, a sarcastic pen, which he used mightily when roused, and an editorial competence which even the rival experts on *The Leeds Mercury* staff did not deny.

The first address of the business was Lowerhead Row, but it was announced in the seventieth number of the *Intelligencer*, on 28 October 1755, that it had been transferred to New Street End, and here it remained until the third decade of the nineteenth century. The *Intelligencer* was not the first Leeds newspaper, for John Hirst, who dwelt 'over against Kirkgate-end' had begun a *Leeds Mercury* in 1718, removing to the 'New Street' in 1731. His successor James Lister carried on the *Mercury* at that address until it expired in 1755, though it was revived in 1767 and rose to great power.

As it is fairly certain that Griffith Wright the elder took over Lister's firm, 'New Street' may be regarded as the cradle of Leeds journalism. The street was situated at the top of Cross Parish, which became known as St John's Street; but even St John's Street is no more. As for New Street End, which joined

Lowerhead Row, it, also, vanished without a trace. The old *Intelligencer* office stood approximately where the present Odeon Cinema now stands.

In the first number of his new paper, the *Intelligencer*'s founder presented his compliments thus:

Whatever may be propos'd for the Support of *Virtue* and *Religion* amongst us, for the Improvement of *Trade* and *Manufactures* of this Part of the Country, for the Encouragement of Industry, the better *Maintenance* or *Employment* of the *Poor*; in short, whatever may *usefully Instruct*, or *innocently Amuse* the Reader, will be suitable *Matter of Intelligence for this Paper*; And whatever is propos'd to this End, in a Way not likely to give *Occasion of Offence*, will be thankfully *receiv'd; and faithfully* and *impartially* communicated to the Public, *By, candid Reader, Your most obedient* humble Servant,

THE PUBLISHER.

But the chief impediments to be encountered were the taxes on paper, on advertisements, and on newspapers as such, duties levied by Governments less desirous of obtaining revenue than of curbing the influence of the Press.

The *Intelligencer* made a modest start. Its first number was a four-page folio containing three columns to a page, and must have cost, though no price is mentioned, not less than 2*d* but not more than 2½*d*. Its contents consisted largely of two staple items: news from the London journals, and advertisements. Among the latter, from the first issue to the last, 1754 to 1866, were puffs for patent medicines of which the paper's proprietors were vendors. During the Wright regime the original day of publication, Tuesday, market day, was changed but once, to Monday; this was done in a year of many changes in the paper, 1792, on 2 January.

It was never a cheap newspaper. By an Act of 1712 a tax of 1*d* had to be paid on every full sheet and ½*d* on every half sheet. Thus when the *Intelligencer* began it paid, in addition to the duties on paper and advertisements, 1*d* duty on each copy and bore for the next hundred years the little red stamp that became so great an object of reproach to those who sought to abolish 'taxes on knowledge'.

In 1777 the price of the *Intelligencer* became 3*d*, as the duty had risen to 1½*d* the year before, and on 4 August 1789 it rose to 3½*d* when the tax went up to 2*d*. By June 1793 the paper increased its price to 4*d* a copy. The newspaper stamp went up again in 1797, to 3½*d*, and in July the *Intelligencer* began to cost 6*d*, but being a loyal paper of the truest blue it thought it idle to complain.

In spite of a rapid increase in the cost of newsprint about the turn of the century, the paper clung to its price of 6*d* until 1809, when, making improvements in its appearance, it felt at last obliged to charge 6½*d* from 28 August. Crippling increases in costs had not yet ended, and in 1815 the newspaper duty was increased to 4*d* a copy and the *Intelligencer* thereupon began to charge 7*d*, the highest price it ever reached.

From the first advertisements were more or less a necessity. They were subject to a duty of 1s each from 1712 to 1757, then of 2s each from 1757 to 1780, of 2s 6d from 1780 to 1789, and, with one of the *Intelligencer*'s rare protests, of 3s until 1815, when it became 3s 6d. Advertisers were never much deterred thereby, but the duty favoured the large advertisement over the small, as it was levied regardless of size.

Social history can be read in the advertisements. These, though apparently of ephemeral interest, are a rich source of information to the local antiquary, who will find among them valuable facts about such matters as sales of property, enclosure commissioners' meetings, the activities of working men's benefit societies, and especially the resolutions of important public meetings, lists of officers of societies and institutions, and prices of various commodities. Information not deemed by the editor to be news of general interest could find a place as advertisement, nor was a Tory paper like the *Intelligencer* above inserting a Whig political advertisement, provided it was paid for. Griffith Wright junior was also agent for a lottery, a form of business that thrives by publicity.

The original format of four pages with three columns to a page was long retained, but while the four pages remained as a folio sheet during the whole Wright regime by judicious rearrangements from time to time much more matter was crammed into the pages. An enlargement took place in 1768, and by 1772, when nearly seven of the paper's sixteen columns were devoted to advertisements, there were four columns a page. When a fifth column was added in May 1792 new Caslon type was introduced on a deeper page. In 1801 smaller and neater type came into use and advertisements were newly laid out.

Bold developments were to come. The year 1809 marks the first great turning point in the paper's history, both in style and content. Six columns were then provided; news and advertisements became so plentiful that in July they even crowded out the title; the title itself was changed to *Wright's Leeds Intelligencer* in August, and the price went up. The paper was responding to political events and strong competition from the *Mercury*, and it took, and needed to take, rapid steps to improve itself.

In March 1811 the first full 'Supplement' came out, new and larger type was employed from January 1812, and a climax was reached in July 1813 with the purchase of a Stanhope press of 'royal' size costing £50. Machine production did not replace the hand press at the *Intelligencer* office for many years yet.

The *Intelligencer* had gradually become a leading Tory newspaper. Originally, Griffith Wright the elder had said that news would be given impartially, and in the eighteenth century his paper was not violently political; it was not violently anything at all, but it displayed a tendency to favour Church, King, and

Constitution. Wright's family were Churchmen, which would predispose them to be Tories also, but in the first fifty years the paper was not more than mildly Pittite and Ministerial.

Real, live squabbling with *The Leeds Mercury* began in earnest in 1806 and continued for forty years with increasing bitterness. The explanation was two-fold: Edward Baines had arrived (he gained control of the *Mercury* in 1801) and

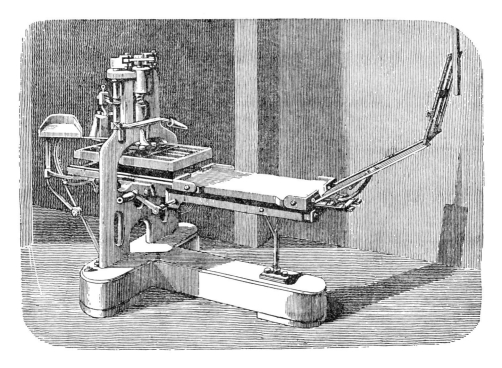

Printing a paper in the days of the hand-operated machine was a laborious affair. Above is an early printing press of the Earl Stanhope type, one of which was bought by
The Leeds Intelligencer *in 1813.*

local industry had taken a new direction. Baines began in 1805 a long period of publicity about his paper which gradually brought him from opponents the title of 'the great liar of the North'. He claimed that the circulation of his *Mercury* was in 1805 far in excess of any other in the town of Leeds (there was but one). The height of fury was reached in 1807–8 during the famous Yorkshire election campaign and its aftermath. There was constant bickering about disloyalty and support of 'Talents' men, Jacobinism and peace at any price by the

Mercury. The mischief-making policy of what the *Intelligencer* styled the 'Orange printer' is summed up thus in May 1808:

The late ostentatious vaunting, puffing and pother of a neighbouring Printer, about himself and his paper, must have strongly reminded his readers of the aspiring bloated frog in the fable . . . And what is the result of all this vain boaster's gasconading? Nothing more than what was before perfectly well known, viz., that the circulation of the 'Mercury' is confined to the disaffected and the illiterate, who are easily misled, deceived and cajoled by flattery and the abuse of their governors.

Wright's asperity cannot conceal the fact that Edward Baines had become a real force in Northern journalism: he was a thorn in the flesh of the *Intelligencer* for the rest of his life.

These were days of industrial changes that led to bitter political strife. The celebrated Yorkshire election of 1807 came when Catholic relief was in the air, but its results turned largely on these industrial questions. As the return of Wilberforce for one of the two seats was regarded as a foregone conclusion, the real contest for the other lay between Lord Milton, Whig, and Lord Lascelles, Tory, and the *Intelligencer*, in supporting Lascelles, took the unpopular side. For Milton obtained his majority, not very large as it turned out, not only at vast expense but also at the cost of promising the small independent manufacturers what he was quite unable to fulfil. Lascelles saw that the future of industry lay with the new and large manufacturers with their machines, which were bound to supersede the individual craftsmen. Milton won, but the arguments about manufacturing methods went on, and in the next election, when it became clear that Lascelles and the *Intelligencer* were right and Milton could do nothing for the small men in spite of his glib promises, Lascelles was returned without opposition. In the same year there came more demonstrative evidence of the small men's opposition to machinery: Luddism. The *Intelligencer* considered that the *Mercury* acted as an 'organ of sedition' at that juncture and never tired of saying so: it was still saying so nearly twenty years later.

The war against Napoleon had given a great fillip to newspapers; the peace of 1815 provided news of equal importance, for 'Reform' was now in the air, with a challenge to the political domination of the landed class, the rising power of industrialists, and the emergence of working-class Radicalism. The old cry of Church and King no longer roused mobs to fury: the growing evils of the factory system did. The *Intelligencer* met special occasions by putting out 'Supplements', for example in December 1816 to give news of the Spa Fields episode.

In March 1817 the publication of a 'Second Edition' is first mentioned; it would be issued, it was announced, if urgent news were received from Manchester about the riots there. It hinted that the *Mercury* belonged to the 'hireling' Press (December 1816) and that Baines himself was an imposter, owning a Whig paper in Leeds and a Tory one in Liverpool. But just at this time Baines scored a signal success over his rival: the *Intelligencer* had stood solidly behind Oliver the Spy and the Government that used such agents; it was Baines who exposed him.

Oliver was employed by the Government to gather information from districts where disturbances were occurring and he manufactured evidence of disaffection by taking the lead in organizing meetings of reformers. On 6 June 1817 he attended one such meeting at Thornhill Lees, near Dewsbury, where he and others taking part were promptly arrested by a strong detachment of soldiers. He was allowed to escape; but this episode led to his undoing. For on 13 June Baines received a letter from a friend who told him that he had heard at Dewsbury that Oliver had tried to entrap a local printer named James Willan into attending the Thornhill Lees meeting.

Baines acted with great promptitude and enterprise. He and his son Edward at once took a chaise to Dewsbury to investigate the facts. Willan told them that Oliver, representing himself as a delegate from Radicals in London, had several times during the past two months tried to incite him into acts of violence, and that he made special efforts to get him to attend the demonstration at which the soldiers had arrested the spy's other dupes. Further inquiries revealed that Oliver had been in touch with the servant of General Byng, the commander of the troops, several days before the meeting. Armed with these facts, Baines returned to Leeds and denounced Oliver in the *Mercury* the following morning as a 'double-distilled traitor' and a 'prototype of Lucifer, whose distinguishing characteristic it is first to tempt and then to destroy'.

In its attention to politics the *Intelligencer* had never neglected other matters likely to interest the public. Whatever the pressure upon its space, it could at all times find room for a good trial, and in its pages may be found records of most human follies and failings, murders, elopements, breaches of promise, and adultery. The higher the station of the persons involved, the more space their misdemeanours got, except, perhaps, in the case of murders, where real equality of opportunity was provided.

For years after its beginning the paper relied to some extent on scissors-and-paste methods in the editorial department. Leading articles were unknown, nor were there any illustrations. From 1785 Parliamentary reports begin to appear and in the early nineteenth century take a prominent place: leading articles are an early nineteenth-century product.

From the first the *Intelligencer* had never been a mere parochial news-sheet:

in the first issue it printed a list of agents who were to be found in various parts of Yorkshire and Lancashire and soon it announced that copies could be seen in London. Its circulation must be reckoned in the early period at hundreds rather than thousands a week, and both gathering of news and distribution of printed copies were attended with difficulties and delays.

Until long after the Wrights had finished with the paper, coaches were the only means of transport of any use to it. Leeds was off the main route to London, and developments in road transport came late to the town. But once begun they made rapid progress. Regular coaches went to London in 1760, one taking a nominal three days, the other two days, going three times a week. The early coach-owners spoke in terms of days; in the 1790's they were talking of hours for this journey. The *Rockingham*, for example, leaving Leeds at 6 am claimed to arrive in London by noon next day.

It was said to have been the intention of the great mail contractor, Palmer, to get the Monday night mail to Leeds by Wednesday morning, but the contractors Gray and Wilson afterwards agreed to do it in twenty-four hours; bad roads defeated this laudable intention, but it has been calculated that the average time taken by mail coaches for a period of thirty years was from thirty to thirty-three hours. By 1836, when coaching days were coming to an end, the time had been reduced to twenty-three hours. Competing coaches raced along; accidents and delays were frequent and caused many anxious moments in the Leeds newspaper offices.

Little is known about the loyal servants who enabled the *Intelligencer* to be produced with such regularity. One old servant, Abraham Nichols, who died in 1807 at the age of 79, had been 'upwards of fifty years in the office of this paper' as printer. By 1819 it is known that regular reporters were employed, and were present at Peterloo (the young Edward Baines of the *Mercury* was certainly there). Hardly anything else is known about the staff, with one exception. His appointment, and the manner of the man himself, mark the beginning of a new regime.

George Mudie, one of the few provincial journalists of this date about whom details have survived, came to Leeds in 1815 to act as editor for Wright after serving for three years with the *Nottingham Gazette*. He quickly made his mark and displayed a talent that might, had he possessed a different temperament, have made him one of the oustanding newspaper editors. In his flamboyant personality, however, a flair for journalism was linked with a love of the good things of life, and he saw that money was to be made in journalism. This led him into a quarrel.

When Wright sold his business at the end of 1818, he intended to hand over

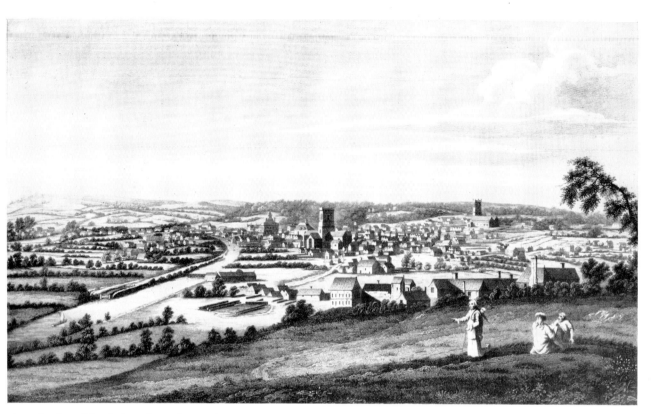

An early view of Leeds from the south-east, from an engraving first reproduced in 1715.
St Peter's Church is in the centre and St John's is on the right.

Leeds from the south-east in 1745, showing the River Aire, St Peter's, Trinity Church, and St John's.

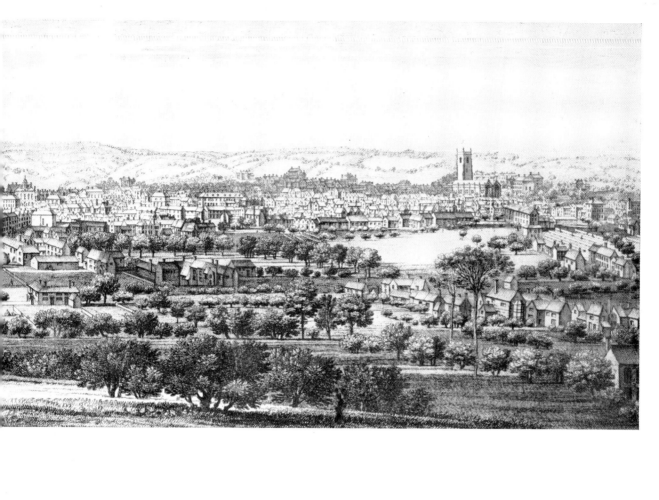

Kirkstall Lock, by J. M. W. Turner (a print of 1827).

The Moot Hall in 1816.
It stood in the centre of Briggate, near the end of Commercial Street, and was demolished in 1825.

to the new proprietors his late editor along with the fixtures and the good-will. But in a farewell message, printed on 14 December 1818, he was obliged to add a note of regret that his editor had violated his agreement. Mudie had decided to set up a paper of his own in partnership with a William Headley. Although this paper, the *Leeds Independent*, lasted seven years, the partnership of these two did not last nine months. It was Mudie who left it. He had behaved foolishly with the firm's money and had been forced to agree to a dissolution under threat of legal proceedings. Matters were eventually settled by arbitration, but not before a long series of accusations and counter-accusations had appeared in the *Intelligencer*, which obligingly inserted them as advertisements. Since the umpire awarded Mudie £1350 it seems that he had a case, however rash his financial transactions might have been. The *Independent* had been a decided success, and he was entitled to a share of the profits since his journalistic skill had contributed much to the paper's rapid progress. No one was readier to pay tribute to his ability than Wright, his former employer. When Mudie edited the *Intelligencer* it made a profit of £1000 a year; after he left the profit fell for a time to £100 a year. But the *Intelligencer* survived to absorb the *Independent* in 1826.

CHAPTER II

Years of change and struggle

[1819–1833]

After Mudie's departure the *Intelligencer* was taken over by a partnership consisting of Thomas Kirkby, William Gawtress, and Thomas Inchbold under the title of Gawtress and Co., which subsisted to sell patent medicines as well as to engage in printing. With the first issue of the new company, on 4 January 1819, the title was changed to *The Leeds Intelligencer and Yorkshire General Advertiser*.

The partnership soon came to grief. Thomas Inchbold was the first to go: he became bankrupt in 1820. But he was a versatile young man and, though ceasing to be a director of the *Intelligencer*, managed to rebuild his fortune and leave behind him the foundations on which the present concern of Beck and Inchbold was reared. He died in the cholera epidemic of 1832. Thomas Kirkby was the sleeping partner, or capitalist, in the scheme. It was he who remained to pay debts and receive dues, if any, when the partnership was finally dissolved in September 1822. The main burden of conducting the paper fell upon Gawtress. He had been established in Leeds for some years as a printer; his principal claim to act as newspaper editor appears to have resided in his skill as a shorthand writer.

Gawtress was said to have made many improvements in the appearance of the *Intelligencer*, but, such as they were, they did not affect it as greatly as those made by his successors. Parliamentary news increased in 1821, editorial comment grew longer, and literary and miscellaneous items on the back page became more plentiful. In his short tenure of office Gawtress had more than his share of special issues, black-lined memorial numbers for members of the Royal family, including King George III. Queen Caroline achieved great notoriety in 1820; column after column was devoted to accounts of her trial. The year following, on 13 August 1821, the *Intelligencer* had to mourn the death of the Queen herself.

A startling issue came out on 27 March 1820 consisting of the four ordinary pages, to which was added a full folio half-sheet, six packed columns to each side, with an account of the trials for sedition of the leading Radicals, Sir Francis Burdett and Henry Hunt.

The names of four of Gawtress's employees have survived. One, John Fothergill, who died in 1851, is not otherwise known; another, James Scott, afterwards became superintendent of the printing department of the Bank of Ireland; a third, Thomas Spirett, was killed in 1854 while on duty tending a machine in the works, having given thirty-five years' service. All these were compositors. In addition there was a 'clerk' called Thomas Wray.

Gawtress took leave of his public on 14 October 1822, with thanks for the indulgence they had shown him in his 'efforts in the cause of social order'. He had tried, he said, to uphold the Constitution and inculcate the Principles of Religion and Loyalty:

He assumed the Management of the *Intelligencer* at a period when Disaffection was rife; when the Revolutionary Mania was advancing with rapid Strides amongst us; and when the Inhabitants of Leeds and the surrounding Districts were suffering under the Pressure of severe Distress; he leaves it in happier Times, in Times of Prosperity and of Peace, but he does so with the Conviction that, should a similar necessity unhappily arise, the *Leeds Intelligencer* will still present a firm Barrier to Innovations which would destroy, whilst they professed to reform, the Constitution; and that the Cause of good Government will obtain in his Successors, *abler*, though he will say, they cannot be more sincere or independent, Advocates.

His financial rewards were meagre. The total profits for the years 1819–22 were only £403.

A vigorous attempt to revive the paper's popularity was made, and needed to be made, by Gawtress's successors: henceforward tenacity, skill, and alertness were vital if the paper were even to survive, let alone make progress. The new proprietors were announced on 14 October 1822 as Robinson and Hernaman, and this combination should have been ideal to put the *Intelligencer* solidly on its feet. It consisted of a prosperous man of business and a first-rate newspaperman.

Joseph Ogle Robinson came of an old Leeds family which had maintained a close connexion with the Leeds Library since its foundation in 1768. Early in the new century the Robinsons moved with the Library into Commercial Street and became its tenants instead of its landlords; it was not surprising, therefore, that the *Intelligencer* soon removed its offices from New Street End thither. A joint office was kept up from October 1822 until September 1824, at which date Commercial Street became the sole address of the *Intelligencer* and so remained to the end of its days.

In view of Robinson's importance in the world of publishing and bookselling it is regrettable that more is not known about him. He went to London to join his fellow 'Yorkshire Tykes' (as Sir Walter Scott called them), Thomas and John Hurst, took over the famous firm of Boydell, and, acting as Constable's London agents, published the most celebrated of the Waverley novels. His connexion with the *Intelligencer* ceased in 1828 and he died in 1837 at the age of 50.

The other partner, John Hernaman, was a newspaper man of considerable ability. He was in control of the paper on the spot. At first all went well and by 1826 he had seen the profits rise to 'twelve times' what they had been in 1819–22, notwithstanding extraordinary expenses in fitting out a new printing office. He was the mainstay of the concern after Robinson's departure and saw the *Intelligencer* through two very anxious years (1828–9), only relinquishing his task in 1832 when he had found an ideal colleague upon whom the paper could depend.

Both proprietors jointly took a decision of great importance in 1822 when they resolved to appoint a first-class editor. They chose Alaric Watts. He was a man of literary ambitions who is remembered now chiefly for his alliterative verses on the siege of Belgrade beginning:

> *An Austrian Army awfully arrayed*
> *Boldly by battery besieged Belgrade.*

His work for journals of various kinds was important at the time not only in content, but in ideas, practice, and aims. At the age of 25, finding that literary work of itself did not yield a living wage, he frankly undertook the editorship of the *Intelligencer* to avoid starvation. He was most generously treated by Robinson and Hernaman, who appointed him at a salary of £300 a year, a higher rate than 'had ever before been paid to the editor of a provincial journal'.

Watts was agreeably surprised by the town of Leeds. Wishing to give the paper 'a more aesthetic and critical character than was then common in the provincial Press' he found that the public responded to his efforts with 'prompt and cordial appreciation'. But there were subscribers who did not prove 'equally progressive in another direction'. A visit to the Infirmary with Michael Thomas Sadler induced him to comment strongly on the inhumanity of the mill-owners: 'on the following Monday he received as many letters discontinuing subscription . . . as filled a breakfast tray'. He met gentlemen and some who were trying to be gentlemen and found some agreeable, some not: Robinson hinted that he should tone down some of his comments on them and refer to everybody in gentlemanly terms, 'except Mr Baines', for whom 'nothing you can say is half bad enough'.

Watts regained the lost subscribers, but soon wearied of his task. His heart

Alaric Watts, editor of The Leeds Intelligencer *from 1822 to 1825.*
(FROM A DRAWING BY DANIEL MACLISE IN FRASER'S MAGAZINE)

was really in London; he was often there, negotiating with Robinson, for example, about the publication of the famous series of Annuals with which his name is associated, or seeking out the literary giants of the day.

In 1825 Watts saw an opening in Manchester and decided to settle there. He established the *Manchester Courier*, but soon tired of that.

A minor crisis in the *Intelligencer*'s affairs occurred from 1828 to 1833, coincident with a major crisis in the history of the Tory Party. There was more coming and going among the partners than usual during 1828 and 1829. First, Robinson's sister, Mary, replaced her brother on 31 July 1828; then, in November Edward Wood was added to the partnership. In May of 1829 it was necessary to deny the truth of a rumour that the paper was about to cease publication; it was also rumoured that Sir John Beckett and M. T. Sadler were going to take it over. In November 1829, Wood departed at the very time when the other two dissolved their own partnership as booksellers. Stabilization was reached on the 'ever memorable November 5th' when the *Intelligencer* was able to address the public about its new proprietors, Hernaman and Perring. They stayed together officially until April 1833 when they separated amicably; Hernaman had in fact left Leeds the year before to start the *Newcastle Journal*. A third partner in the enterprise was William Thomas Bolland, a Leeds iron-master, but he remained very much in the background and his connexion with the *Intelligencer* was not disclosed until Perring left in 1842.

About Perring more must be said presently. Mary Robinson died on 15 January 1850 in her seventy-third year. Wood's career is obscure: he was on the staff of the paper in 1824, but the one fact that has secured him a small niche in history is that little Charlotte Brontë knew him as (or thought he was) editor of the paper to which her father contributed letters on the Roman Catholic Relief question and on the bog eruptions at Haworth.

The rivalry between the *Intelligencer* and the *Mercury* was at its bitterest during the years from 1822 to 1833. Watts was soon at loggerheads with Baines and by March 1824 had sued him for libel. The *Mercury* had printed abusive personal comments on Watts and his ability and Watts sought retribution at the Yorkshire Spring Assizes. The result was a technical defeat for Baines, who had to pay the costs of both sides, but the damages awarded, a sum of one shilling, were insufficient to restrain him from resuming his attacks. Watts was his equal in outspokenness and mutual recriminations occupied much space in the papers during the month of April 1824.

Further trouble occurred in 1827. In November a case was tried which concerned the profits of the *Intelligencer*, already mentioned, and was commented upon by Baines. In reply to his reflections on the sad state the paper had reached, the *Intelligencer* responded with warmth that what had happened between 1819 and 1822 bore no relation to what had happened in the following six years:

As well might we say that the portly proprietor of the Mercury – the Sexagenarian dandy of Briggate – the Solon of the Leeds Workhouse – the Demosthenes of the Hunslet rabble – the father of Talbot Baines, Esq., the barrister-at-law – the sire of that *sola voluptas*, the travelled Adonis – and the lord of the manor of a piece of Lancashire moss . . . is still the same poverty-stricken adventurer that he was thirty years ago, when he wandered into Leeds, his whole fortune centered in a 'composing stick' and his head as empty of learning as his back was bare of clothes.

It did not wish to follow Baines's good advice: it would pursue a High Tory policy:

But alas we have not been *moderate* like the Mercury. We certainly have not: nor do we believe that, till lately, moderation was a virtue in that quarter. It was not, we imagine, over mild for Mr Baines to summon, every Friday, during Lord Sidmouth's Administration of the Home Department, a conclave of his wiser patrons in this town, and submit to them the articles prepared for the ensuing day's paper in order to ascertain the utmost degree of treason which might be published with the least risk of the gallows.

Baines's agitation for reform had been a cover for keeping the town in terror of insurrectionary mobs, it added, a policy he pursued with exultation till the Acts of 1819 silenced the country's traitors.

But throughout the decade Baines contined confident. He was on the winning side: not only was his paper making rapid progress, but the Tories were on the retreat. Whatever efforts the *Intelligencer* made to thunder its party propaganda, Baines and his fellows were irresistible. First they succeeded in capturing for John Marshall of Leeds, a Whig, a Unitarian, and a manufacturer, one of the Yorkshire seats at the county election in 1826; it was Baines more than anyone who had performed what was considered the miracle of putting a tradesman into a place hitherto reserved exclusively for a landed gentleman.

Then, in 1830, it was what was called the 'Bainesocracy' that procured the return of Brougham for Yorkshire, to the chagrin not only of the Tories, who could not be expected to love a Whig place-seeker who was not even a Yorkshireman, but of the Whig aristocracy themselves, who resented the interference of Mr Edward Baines and the West Riding manufacturing interest. To crown their series of brilliant successes, Baines and his followers succeeded in defeating the Tory candidate, M. T. Sadler, in the first Leeds Parliamentary election of 1832.

The year 1828 had seemed to be the beginning of the end for the Tory party. Concessions had been made to dissenters that year, followed by Roman Catholic

Relief in 1829; agitation for the Reform Bill had begun; the Leeds Pitt Club finished its career and the new Brunswick Club was no adequate substitute. It was true that the Tories had taken up the cause of the working man, but ordinary working men did not possess the vote. Baines had wooed the working-class Radicals and won them to his side for a time; but gradually they saw that the *Intelligencer* was right in its contention that the Whigs were their flatterers and not their true friends. On one occasion they burned Baines in effigy outside his own office: Baines accused Thomas Inchbold of supplying the trousers.

The new alliance of Tory and Radical is personified in the figure of Richard Oastler. Every student of social history knows (for his text-books tell him) that Oastler's famous letter on 'Yorkshire Slavery' first appeared in *The Leeds Mercury* of 16 October 1830. It is far less well known that Baines quickly tired of Oastler's vociferous attacks on the mill-owners (who were, after all, Baines's allies), cut down a fourth letter on the factory question, and then saw it appear in full in the rival *Intelligencer*. Thereafter it was the *Intelligencer* that consistently backed Oastler's cause, became his firm friend, and retained his affection to the end of his days.

Just at the time when a London paper proclaimed that 'Toryism is dead in Yorkshire', there was a spirited revival. A True Blue Society was formed in Leeds with Henry Hall of the old guard at its head, and in reporting its proceedings the *Intelligencer* used for the first time in Leeds the new label Conservative Party. This was on 17 May 1832.

Throughout this period the price of the *Intelligencer* remained constant at 7*d*, for no relief had yet come from any of the three taxes. The day of publication was changed from Monday to Thursday on 2 January 1823, and so remained until 23 February 1833. The intention in 1823 was to avoid the 'disagreeable alternative of infringing on the duties of the Sabbath'. The change was made not merely out of solicitude for the staff, but to conform to the strictness of Sunday observance then growing in Leeds. The Baines family were extremely dutiful in this respect.

The size of the paper was enlarged on 4 January 1827 and widened to contain seven columns on 24 May 1832. New types were introduced on 21 July 1825. In the absence of figures, it can only be said that the *Intelligencer* was not in such a flourishing condition as its chief rival in Leeds. It now had to suffer the first stages of competition from other rivals. Not reckoning Mudie's ill-fated *Gazette*, two new papers, longer but not very much longer lived, began to appear in Leeds: the *Independent*, which ceased in 1826, and the *Leeds Patriot*, which began in 1824. One small accession to the *Intelligencer*'s strength was made in April 1828 by the incorporation of the *Bradford Courier*. By 1831 its circulation was about 1500 copies a week.

CHAPTER III

'The Altar, the Throne, and the Cottage'

[1833–1866]

As it entered on its final period, the *Intelligencer* gained an editor of outstanding character. Robert Perring was a native of Carlisle and had served as editor of the *Carlisle Patriot*, a paper in which the Lowthers took a close interest, since its start in 1815. The reader of the *Intelligencer* during his editorship feels that he is in contact with a man of restless vigour, and Perring had need of all the energy he could muster. It was not only that he made technical alterations in the paper; he gave it an argumentative tone it very much needed to counter the work of the Baines family. What really mattered was that he kept the paper alive when it might very well have gone under. For seven very difficult years he strove to make it a first-class paper in the Conservative interest.

At the end of 1840 it was decided to put out an additional paper, 'on sound Conservative principles', which would bridge the gap between the Saturday issues of the *Intelligencer*. On 6 January 1841 there duly appeared the first number of the *Leeds Wednesday Journal*, at 4d 'ready money' or 5s a quarter 'on credit'. It had a modest circulation and a short life, expiring on 24 February of the same year. Whether by coincidence or not, its publication marks the end of Perring's service with the *Intelligencer*. His retirement from the post of editor was announced on 19 February 1842, along with a statement, to set rumours at rest, that the separation had been by mutual consent. This is hard to believe, for he set up a rival firm at 23 Commercial Street, only four doors away, to publish the *Leeds Conservative Journal*. This, again, had but a brief existence, running from 7 May to 24 September.

Perring served for a time on one or more of the London papers, but returned to Carlisle in 1848 to resume the editorship of the *Patriot* he had relinquished thirty-three years before. He died on 4 October 1869 in his eighty-second year. Three years earlier his paper had been taken over by the Carlisle Conservative

Newspaper Company and the *Intelligencer* had become the property of the Yorkshire Conservative Newspaper Company.

Although Perring indulged in miscellaneous printing, just as his predecessors had done, his life-work was newspaper editing. His deep interest in his profession is shown by the fact that he was one of a body of editors from the provinces who went to interview the Chancellor of the Exchequer in April 1836 about matters concerning the welfare of the Press. It was a momentous occasion for the profession; for before they returned home these delegates, Baines among them, founded the Provincial Newspaper Society. Baines was an original Vice-President and second President in 1837-8; Perring was the fifth President, in 1840-1.

His time as editor in Leeds was one of great political ferment, full of challenge for the journalist. He had to do battle with the Whigs in power, both locally and nationally: he had to contend with the reactions of the country to a constitutional revolution.

One illustration of the trouble Perring had with the Whigs in power must suffice. It involved his paper in much difficulty and cost. Two constables doing their duty in a street fight in Leeds had been accused of assault. The one appointed by the Court Leet had been fined; the other, whose appointment had been approved by the new Whig magistrates, had been let off. This discrimination angered Perring. In November 1836 he accused three Leeds magistrates, Clapham, Musgrave, and Darnton Lupton, whom he consistently referred to as 'Russell magistrates', of 'unblushingly sacrificing the duties of their office to party purposes'. They took prompt action and the case of King v. Perring came up for hearing in the Court of King's Bench on 30 January 1837. A rule *nisi* for a criminal information was obtained, but nothing more was heard of the case until 24 May the following year. Sir William Follett then showed cause against the rule and the Attorney-General appeared in support of the rule, but the Court thought it should be discharged on the defendant paying costs; otherwise it would be made absolute.

Perring refused to pay; the plaintiffs, he said, could go on; they had put him already to an expense of £200; their real object was to curb the Press, but they would find it too strong for them. They would be wise, he suggested, to be satisfied with the £230 costs they had put him to, 'punishment enough for the mighty offence of questioning the correctness of a decision by which one person is virtually acquitted and yet convicted and fined, and by which another person, though equally participating in all that was done, is not even charged but let off out of respect, he being of the Justices' own political colour'. In spite of this outspoken reiteration of his charge, the justices took his advice and did not proceed.

The forthright Perring also joined battle on behalf of the Press for the right to report the proceedings in the Town Council. The new councillors showed some reluctance to have their speeches reported: they would admit reporters, they said, on the understanding that they might be expelled, without reason given, at any time. Did these councillors, Perring retorted, think they could curb the freedom of the Press by such a 'side-wind' intimidation which was really a threat to editors? They mistook their power – the Press was stronger than they – they would not dare to close their doors and carry on discussions in secret. It was not his only clash with the Council, but he stood his ground, and over the years provided his readers with very full reports.

Perring gave the paper a motto which summarized its aims: 'The Altar, the Throne, and the Cottage'. More elaborately, he said in his New Year message for 1838, for example:

We are Constitutional and Conservative – attached to the Monarchy and the Church: and while we contend for the independence and efficiency of the House of Peers, we are equally desirous of promoting the independence and efficiency of the House of Commons. We would apply the hand of reform wherever reform is really wanted.

The important word was 'really'; to reform must not be to destroy. The 'Cottage' in the motto represented the Tory-Radical alliance (exemplified by the co-operation between Oastler and M. T. Sadler), and Perring lent support to the Leeds Operative, that is working-men's, Conservative Society, founded in 1835, largely at the instance of William Beckwith and William Paul. His speech at its dinner on 25 November 1835 put the Society on its feet.

Perring had other political troubles. It was not merely that the Conservative cause was then in a decline in the West Riding, nor yet that he saw the *Mercury* 'a swellin' wisibly before his wery eyes'; all that was bad enough, but new and vigorous competitors emerged after the reduction of the stamp duty on newspapers. A great war for circulation followed.

The *Leeds Times* had been established in March 1833, and after a shaky start soon reached the output of the *Intelligencer* and even, in one year (1837), exceeded it. Then in November of the latter year the *Northern Star* appeared on the scene and with a meteoric rise not only outshone the *Intelligencer*, the *Mercury*, and the *Leeds Times*, but in 1839 had a circulation more than twice that of all three put together.

This illustrates the rapid expansion of the demand for the Radical journals. It was a hard fight, but Perring substantially increased the circulation of his paper. He also maintained its prestige as the leading Conservative organ in Yorkshire, and so was able to claim that it was a first-class advertising medium.

The duty on advertisements continued at its maximum rate of 3*s* 6*d* each, but it only deterred the small advertiser. In one issue, for example, that of 11 June 1836, eighteen out of thirty-two columns consisted of advertisements.

Perring changed the day of publication in February 1833 to Saturday, not merely because that day was market day, with obvious advantages, but because by some kind of 'hocus-pocus', which he could not get to the bottom of, it so happened that most local, and even national meetings seemed to be held on Thursdays, just after the *Intelligencer* had gone to press and been sent out, but just in time to allow the *Mercury* to get the cream of the news. Work had to start

A Napier-type printing press.

on the final printing early on Friday afternoon to allow distribution to distant subscribers on Saturday, but the practice was adopted at this time of issuing regularly three or four editions with later news inserted on the middle page.

Whether from jealousy, lack of resources, or real contempt, the *Intelligencer* was always shy of using illustrations and mocked Baines for so doing in imitation of the *Northern Star*; but it followed the fashion on rare occasions itself. Pictures of the latest ladies' fashions in April and May 1840 were a distinct innovation. Supplements or 'extraordinary' sheets were put out on special occasions. In 1836 improvements in typography were introduced when a

'Desideratum Machine' of David Napier's invention was installed. This could throw off 900 copies an hour in an emergency, but its average output was 700 or 800 copies. Its real significance, marking its acquisition as a distinct milestone in the paper's history, was that it was driven by steam.

Railway expansion was now at its height, and Perring's editorship was a real time of transition in means of communication. He had still to depend largely on coaches for his mail, though the new railways were making rapid progress. In 1835 he proudly printed the following:

Rapid Circulation of News – By an express from the Sun Office, the result of the divisions on Lord John Russell's resolution which took place in the Commons on Friday morning at 3 o'clock reached the newspaper offices in Leeds by 1 o'clock on Saturday, and the Resignation of Ministers, with a full report of his speech delivered in the House of Commons between five and six o'clock on Wednesday evening, was known in Leeds soon after noon on Thursday. These are astonishing as well as very costly exertions and the public would be insensible indeed were it not to appreciate them as they deserve.

In 1837 the Grand Junction Railway reached Manchester from London, the journalist's Mecca, whereupon the businessmen of Leeds, with Perring to the fore, anxiously debated how that quicker means of communication could be used in conjunction with a re-timed coach from Manchester to Leeds. In 1840 their hopes were realized and Leeds and London at last were linked by rail direct.

The carriage of newspapers by post is one of the curiosities of economic history. In return for the stamp duty they were allowed to circulate free of cost within the limits of the G.P.O. not only once, but as many times, on being re-addressed, as was consistent with the paper holding together. The system was to outlast Perring and the *Intelligencer* itself, but he was able to see the abolition of many anomalies and the introduction of a uniform penny-post by Sir Rowland Hill in 1840 after making his own efforts to secure them.

In 1838 he had a staff of thirty-eight. Most of them are utterly forgotten now, but his chief reporter is well known: he was the excellent John Beckwith, who afterwards became the Clerk to the Leeds Board of Guardians. He joined the staff in 1825 and died in 1856. Another reporter for a short time was Kitchen, who emigrated to Australia in 1840 and achieved the reputation of being 'the most talented' newspaper editor there before he died in 1852. The chief press-men were Thomas and John Spirett, the 'overseer' was P. G. Townsend, the assistant publisher J. Wallis, and George Kitson and W. A. Legg were clerks at the 'compting house'.

In the last stage of its career, the *Intelligencer* was in the hands of a man who, combining scholarly tastes with a deep love of journalism, was a praiseworthy, if not great, editor. In his staid and capable charge it finished its career without glory, but without indiginity. It could not compare with the *Mercury* in thrust and vigour, but it did its work honestly and with competence. But by 1866 the days of weekly newspapers were numbered if they wished to remain effective over more than a restricted area.

In January 1841, W. T. Bolland senior had at last openly joined a partnership in which he had long wielded power. When Perring withdrew a year later, Bolland took a new partner on 7 May 1842 and the firm became Bolland and Kemplay. Six years later to the week, Bolland withdrew and substituted his son, also named William Thomas, but the firm's title became significantly, Kemplay and Bolland. In April 1848 Kemplay was left to rule alone, after an amicable dissolution of partnership. For almost a quarter of a century, therefore, the direction of the paper was virtually his, at least on the editorial side.

Christopher Kemplay, the son of a Leeds schoolmaster, was born in 1804 and was educated at his father's school and at Ripon Grammar School. He was interested in literary and scientific studies and early took up writing. This led to his appointment as editor of the *Yorkshire Gazette*. But though this post took him to York he never lost his connexion with Leeds; for he was invited on several occasions to lecture to the Leeds Philosophical and Literary Society between 1831 and 1841. Two of these lectures were on subjects that were of life-long interest to him: smoke and comets. He published a book on the latter topic in 1859 and was founder of the first and short-lived Leeds Astronomical Society, established in that year and only revived a generation later. He held office in various other societies and institutions, particularly the Mechanics' Institute, and was a churchwarden of St John's, Briggate, Leeds. His home was within a stone's throw of the church. He died in his sixty-eighth year on 26 May 1872, and was buried at Chapel Allerton.

He was almost morbidly afraid of giving offence and successfully kept his paper and himself out of the law courts. He took great care to preserve anonymity and frowned upon the practice often adopted by Sir Edward Baines of signing articles over his own name. His leading articles are many, often long, and excellently written.

In many ways the *Intelligencer* began to assume the appearance of its modern successor: Kemplay started a 'Correspondent's Letter' from London; he gave great prominence to agriculture; music was always fully reported; sporting news gradually increased; a vast amount of commercial intelligence was printed; and church affairs were always fully reported. Earlier editors had not been fond of illustrations: the Crimean war led to the publication of many drawings of the Crimea. Books were regularly reviewed, even magazines, and he always provided a large selection of 'Miscellaneous' items of the widest possible interest. His aim was to produce a paper fit for a gentleman's table that would not disgrace the Victorian ideal of domesticity; but on occasion he could print exceedingly long, detailed reports of scandalous misconduct.

When he took charge the paper still cost $4\frac{1}{2}d$ for eight folio pages. By 1853, when the war in the Crimea broke out, the eight pages had become twelve, and at the beginning of 1854 the price was reluctantly raised to 5d. One relief came in 1853 with the abolition of the tax on advertisements in August; another in July 1855, when the second and greatest of the 'taxes on knowledge', that on newspapers as such, ceased on 30 June. In consequence the *Mercury* now began to appear as a tri-weekly and the *Intelligencer*, for a time, as a bi-weekly.

The new arrangement did not last long, for the *Intelligencer* reverted to its weekly single appearance after Saturday, 29 March 1856, but included the four-page supplement to give a total of twelve pages. Even this reversion was amended after 1 January 1859, when the 'Supplement' disappeared and the paper came out in larger form at 3d a copy, unstamped, or 4d stamped.

In 1861 the third and last of the taxes came to an end, celebrated by the *Intelligencer* of 5 October by a special article on the 'Emancipation of the Press' and an announcement that on and after that date the price would be only 2d unstamped and 3d stamped. So it remained to the end: the final number of Saturday, 30 June 1866 appeared still as an eight-page paper, still priced 2d (or 3d stamped), and still with the address at 19 Commercial Street. Events were proving that the situation could not be allowed to rest there: Kemplay himself might still be content to remain in his old happy rut, but since October 1861 the Liberal *Mercury* had begun to appear as a daily paper, a distinct challenge to Conservatives which was not long declined.

A new England was emerging, an era of 'progress' and prosperity. During his editorship, Kemplay saw Chartism rise and fall; he did not like it and rejoiced at the collapse of its militant supporters because they had threatened the balance of powers in the State. He saw the great peace broken by the Crimean War: he detested the Government that had blundered and blustered its way into it. He saw the triumph of Free Trade, but warned his readers about the 'Nemesis of Agitation'. He saw Wellington and Peel depart, the old Toryism decline, and the Peelites disintegrate. These and other events are part of English history. Three names were anathema to Kemplay: those of Lord John Russell, Richard Cobden, and Sir Edward Baines. They personified all the things the *Intelligencer* abhorred: 'Whig jiggery-pokery in high places'; Free Trade and Peace at any Price; and Liberal Infallibility and the Dissidence of Dissent.

In October 1848 the *Sheffield Mercury* shocked Conservatives by going over 'bag and baggage' to the Liberal camp. Thereupon the *Intelligencer* began to provide Sheffield with the Conservative news of which it had been deprived. A transition was reached in November of that year when Edmund Denison, described as a Liberal-Conservative, was returned for the West Riding to the joy of the *Intelligencer*, which saw in the result proof positive that Baines and Carbutt, of Leeds, did not preside over the destinies of the Riding, and told them so. Denison was the sixth son of Sir John Beckett, Bt, but took the name of Denison in 1816. He resumed his family surname when he succeeded to the baronetcy. His fellow M.P. was a misguided gentleman, whom Kemplay took to calling the 'accidental Member' for the West Riding, in contrast to the real or Peelite Member. This was Richard Cobden.

Kemplay also saw a Conservative revival in Leeds; and not before time. The climax came in 1852 when, after Kemplay had long tried to rouse local Conservatives to resist Whig dominance in political affairs, the Parliamentary election came upon them and found them asleep. The Liberals had neither slumbered nor slept. They had so successfully laboured that it was deemed useless to oppose their candidates, Sir George Goodman and M. T. Baines. This was more than the *Intelligencer* could stand. Were the voters of Leeds to be denied the pleasure of a contested election for the first time since 1832? At the very last moment two Conservative candidates were found, but it was far too late in the day: they stood no chance of election. The episode had come as a much-needed tonic and Kemplay hammered the lesson home. The Conservatives set to work to organize an efficient party machine. Kemplay had not spoken in vain.

While political matters were still, naturally, the life-blood of a Conservative newspaper, the *Intelligencer* occupied itself a great deal with the stirrings of the Victorian conscience about the great 'social' question. This might be the age of the Great Exhibition and such enterprises as the Leeds Chamber of Commerce, but it was also the age of cholera, slums, and neglect of education. Kemplay gave a large amount of space to the valiant attempt to clean up England in general and Leeds in particular.

The cholera epidemic of 1849, following the menace of Chartism, shook any complacency that remained. It gave Leeds a shock it did not forget. Opposition to the great cost of adequate sewerage was gradually overcome. Old, and even new, burial grounds were ordered to be closed. Overcrowding was exposed, model 'cottages' for the worker were strongly advocated, especially Denison's ideal lodging house, a vigorous campaign was launched to secure Woodhouse Moor ('the lungs of Leeds', Baines called it) as an open space for ever. The

The first office of The Leeds Intelligencer – *from 1754 to 1824 – was in the building that later became Bean's bookshop, at New Street End next to the old Corn Exchange. This is where the Odeon Cinema now stands.*

In 1822 The Leeds Intelligencer *established an office in Commercial Street, in the buildings now occupied by the Leeds Library. From 1824 to 1866 this was the sole home of the paper.*

THE
LEEDES INTELLIGENCER.

Printed by GRIFFITH WRIGHT, in the LOWER-HEAD-ROW.

N° 1. TUESDAY, *July* 2, 1754.

The PUBLISHER's PREFACE.

THO' from the Abundance of Materials in the public Prints, a Weekly Collection of News may be made that will answer the Printer's Intention; yet it cannot be doubted, that an Undertaking of this Kind wou'd be much more *Useful* and *Entertaining*, if it was made a Means of establishing a *public* and *friendly* Correspondence, amongst Gentlemen and Others, who have apply'd themselves with some Degree of Attention to any Branch of Science or Business in the Neighbourhood.

It is surprising to observe, and yet every thinking Man has in many Instances observ'd, from what *slender Hints* have been produc'd the most *useful Improvements* in the several Trades and Occupations, which are the Support and Ornament of human Society. And there are perhaps but few Men of good natural Parts and Understanding, who have not form'd in their own Minds, some imperfect Schemes for the Improvement of the Business they are engag'd in, which yet, for want of seeing their full Tendency, or for want of Ability in themselves to put them in Execution, they have utterly neglected as useless or impracticable. Now if *Schemes* of this Kind were freely communicated, and candidly examin'd and compar'd, by Persons concern'd in the same Branch of Business; it can hardly be suppos'd but the Result of such a Precedure, wou'd always be something of *singular Advantage to the Public*.

With regard more especially to the *Trade* and *Manufactures* of this Part of the Country, wherein Gentlemen of great Capacity, of enlarg'd Understanding and unwearied Application are engag'd; such an Intercourse as is here propos'd, wou'd in all Probability be attended with Success, even beyond what the liveliest Imagination can at present conceive; for considering what Improvements in the several Branches of Business have been made of late by *meer Chance*, by some lucky Hit, and in a Manner without any View or Design to such Improvements; very great Advantages wou'd most certainly be made, and our Expectations of Success could hardly be raised too high, if Gentlemen of *Sagacity* and *Penetration*, assisted by a special Knowledge and Experience in the different Branches of Trade, were jointly to apply their Attention to this Purpose.

Projects intirely new have indeed thro' various unforeseen Difficulties and Hazards, been attended oftentimes with fatal Miscarriages; but Attempts to improve upon o'd Inventions, are by no Means liable to the same Dangers, and are moreover better adapted to what is observ'd to be the distinguishing Characteristic of the *British* Genius. And besides the real Advantages which may be expected from the different *Schemes*, *Proposals*, *Dissertations*, *&c.* to this Purpose; the Entertainment likewise, will be much greater to every Reader in this Neighbourhood, than can possibly be had from the repeated Accounts given us in the public News Papers of the continu'd Squabbles between the Subjects of his *Holiness*, and his Most Christian Majesty in *France*; the lamentable Devastations made by Incendaries in *Muscovy*; or the different Successes of the several Pretenders to the Throne of *Persia*.

Gentlemen, who whether thro' the Sufficiency of their Acquisitions, or their love of Retirement have declin'd Business, might with great Satisfaction to Themselves, and inconceivable Advantage to the Public, employ some of their leisure Hours in suggesting to their Successors and others in Trade, and Suggestions of this Kind wou'd come with a peculiar Grace and Energy from those who had so largely experienc'd and observ'd the Success of them; that *Honesty is the best Policy*; that Artifice and Fraud give but vanishing and delusive Prospects of Advantage, and are in reality, sooner or later, the never-failing Ruin of Commerce; that Ingenuity and Fair dealing are the only sure and lasting Supports of Credit; and that however the HONOUR OF TRADE, as it is call'd, may preserve the Appearance, yet an uniform Course of Uprightness and Fidelity, of Generosity and Benevolence, which render a Tradesman a Blessing to his Country, can only be expected to be maintain'd on its true Foundation of *Conscience* and *Religion*.

The Interests of *Virtue* and *Religion* might likewise this Way be serv'd in various other Instances which are probably thought not of Importance enough, or which upon some Account or other, it seems, are thought not proper to be taken notice of from the Pulpit.

By this *public Correspondence*, some *Discovery* perhaps might be made of the *real Views* and *Designs* of a Body of Men lately settl'd amongst us, who are united amongst themselves, and secluded as much as may be from the rest of the World, no less by the Ties of Commerce, than by the peculiar Tenets of Religion they maintain; whether their Trade be intended for the Support and Encouragement of their religious Peculiarities; or their Professions of Religion are made for a *cover* and *disguise* to some *artful* and *fraudulent* Designs in Trade; in short, whether they are to be look'd upon with a jealous and watchful Eye, or deserve to be countenanc'd and encourag'd as Friends and Benefactors to the Country.

By such a *Communication of Intelligence* as is here propos'd, a fair Opportunity wou'd be given of removing, in good Time, those popular Jealousies and Surmises, which are apt to arise on the approaching Commencement of any *New Laws*; and which, whether they be the natural Effects of that *Liberty* we so justly boast of, or be industriously raised by mischievous and ill-designing Persons, might easily be remov'd, and the real Patriotism and Benevolence of the Undertaking wou'd excite any one, who is qualify'd, to Attempt the Removal of *these Evils* by a proper Explanation of such Laws. And *real Grievances*, if such were at any Time justly apprehended, might in this Way likewise be so *modestly* and *clearly* represented, as to be immediately prevented or redress'd by the Authority of Those who are intrusted with the Execution of Laws, or by their Application to the *Legislature*; which is indisputably the farthest of any in the World from singling out any Body of Men, or any particular Person as a Mark of Oppression.

Accounts of *Occurrences*, *&c.* in the Neighbourhood, whether *serious* or *jocose*, of our *rural Diversions*, their Use and Intention, how far the Intention is answer'd, and the like, wou'd be more Entertaining to the Generality of Readers in the Country, than any Thing we have yet heard of the *Routs*, *Riots*, *Drums*, and *Hurricanes* of the Town: And perhaps it may be thought a Point of Prudence to suspend our Approbation of these noisy Diversions, and utterly to discountenance their Admission amongst us, at least till we be pretty well assur'd that they are the genuine Product and Invention of a truly judicious and refin'd Taste, and not an awkward or burlesque Imitation only of the *Romps and Gambols of a Country Wake*.

Whatever may be propos'd for the Support of *Virtue* and *Religion* amongst us, for the Improvement of the *Trade* and *Manufactures* of this Part of the Country, for the Encouragement of *Industry*, the better *Maintenance* or *Employment* of the *Poor*; in short, whatever may *usefully Instruct*, or *innocently Amuse* the Reader, will be *suitable Matter of Intelligence for this Paper*. And whatever is propos'd to this End, in a Way not likely to give any *Occasion of Offence*, will be *thankfully receiv'd*; and *faithfully* and *impartially* communicated to the Public.

By, candid Reader, Your
most obedient,
humble Servant,
The PUBLISHER

Friday's POST.

From the LONDON PRINTS, June 25.

☞ *Arriv'd the* MAILS *from* FRANCE *and* HOLLAND.

Posnania, [*a City of Great* Poland] *June* 5.

THE Forest near Sierzky being set on Fire by accident, the Space of a whole Mile was reduced to Ashes.

Berlin, [*Capital of* Prussia] *June* 11. They write from Ziethen, that on the 5th Inst. about nine in the Evening, there was seen there a fiery Meteor in the Shape of a Musket, which proceeded from the Planet Venus, and ran in a direct Line towards the Earth. Several loud Claps, like the Noise of a Cannon, were heard at the same Time, which made the People apprehensive of a Storm. This Flame was succeeded by a clear white Ray, in a straight Line, and of a considerable Length, which following the Flame, and being directly under Venus as far as could be perceived, entered into that Planet, and occasioned a Smoke like that of a Chimney. The Smoke, which came away in a serpentine Form, continued visible near a Quarter of an Hour. This Meteor was also seen in this City, but we did not hear the Claps.

Hanover, [*a City of* Germany] *June* 9. Lord Berkeley and his Lady who arrived here last Monday, as also the Duke of Richmond and his Brother Lord George Lenox, are treated with particular Marks of Distinction. Yesterday these illustrious Foreigners were carried to Herrenhausen in a Phaeton belonging to the Court, drawn by six Horses; and the Grand Jet d'Eau played for their Entertainment, for the first Time this Season.

Francfort, [*a City of* Germany] *June* 12. The Scarcity of Corn is so great in the Circle of Franconia, particularly in the Bishoprics of Wurtzbourg and Bamberg, that whole Families of Persons in good Circumstances have had no Bread to eat for eight Days. The Poor of this City continue to be supplied by the Magistrates out of the public Magazines.

Paris, [*Capital of* France] *June* 12. While the Nation is in Expectation of seeing the Parliament of the Metropolis speedily recalled, the Deputies about the Bull Unigenitus begin to subside in several Dioceses. At Orleans, two Prebendaries who had been expelled the Choir by the late Bishop, have again taken their Seats, from a Persuasion that such an Exclusion ought not to be in Force under the new Bishop. In effect, this Prelate having assisted at the Choir in the Whitsun-holydays, one of the two Prebendaries staid there: The other did not stay, but told the Dean of the Chapter that he supposed it could be of no Consequence, as he thought himself clearly entitled to stay if he pleased. To which the Dean answered, that he was in the right, and that he himself was to blame for not having informed them that the Bishop had declared, some Time before Penticost, that it was his Intention to avoid every Thing that might set him at variance with his Chapter.

The new Bishop of Evreux, Successor of the Prelate whose Conduct so highly irritated the Parliament of Normandy, has declared to his Synod, that he will not allow the Clergy under his Jurisdiction to talk to the Laity about the Bull Unigenitus, or the other Matters which occasion Disputes in the Church. And the Count de St. Florentin, Secretary of State, has wrote a very polite Letter to the Chapter of Auxerre, importing, that the King will soon appoint a Bishop to that Diocese, and that in the mean Time his Majesty desires the Chapter to be careful to preserve the same Tranquility which prevailed there under the late Bishop.

Paris, *June* 14. By the Repairs and Preparation, making at the Palace, the speedy Return of the Parliament seems beyond all question. M. de Maupeau upon his return to Soissons, made it his first Business to inform the exiled Members dispersed in several Parts of the Country, of his Majesty's gracious Intention to terminate himself those Affairs which gave occasion to the removal of the Parliament.

It is just declared, that the Letters de Cachet for the recall of the Parliament are signed and sent away to the several Places whither the Members are exiled; but such is the Exultation of the Publick, that not a few seemed backward to believe it. This most happy Event is owing to the Prince of Conti and the Marshals Noailles and Belleisle.

Hague, [*in* Holland] *June* 19. The Earl of Cardigan and Lord Brudenel, with their Ladies, and several other Persons of Distinction, are arrived here

The first Leeds Intelligencer: *July 2, 1754.*

GLORIOUS VICTORY
OVER THE
Combined Fleets of France & Spain!

DEATH of LORD NELSON.

From the London Gazette Extraordinary.

Admiralty-Office, November 6.

DISPATCHES, of which the following are copies, were received at the Admiralty this day at one o'clock A.M. from Vice-Admiral Collingwood, Commander in Chief of His Majesty's ships and vessels off Cadiz:

Euryalus, off Cape Trafalgar, Oct. 22.

SIR,—The ever to be lamented death of Vice-Admiral Lord Viscount Nelson, who, in the late conflict with the enemy, fell in the hour of victory, leaves, to me the duty of informing my Lords Commissioners of the Admiralty, that on the 19th inst. it was communicated to the Commander in Chief from the ships watching the motions of the enemy in Cadiz, that the combined fleet had put to sea; as they sailed with light winds westerly, his Lordship concluded their destination was the Mediterranean, and immediately made all sail for the Streights' entrance, with the British squadron, consisting of 27 ships, three of them 64's where his Lordship was informed by Capt. Blackwood, (whose vigilance in watching and giving notice of the enemy's movements, has been highly meritorious) that they had not yet passed the Streights.

On Monday the 21st inst. at daylight, when Cape Trafalgar bore E. by S. about seven leagues, the enemy was discovered six or seven miles to the Eastward, the wind

To the Right Hon. Rear Admiral the Earl of Northesk, to the Captains, Officers and Seamen, and to the Officers, Non-commissioned Officers, and Privates of the Royal Marines, I beg to give my sincere and hearty thanks for their highly meritorious conduct, both in the action, and in their zeal and activity in bringing the captured ships out from the perilous situation in which they were, after their surrender, among the shoals of Trafalgar, in boisterous weather. And I desire that the respective Captains will be pleased to communicate to the Officers, Seamen and Royal Marines this public testimony of my high approbation of their conduct, and my thanks for it.

C. COLLINGWOOD.

GENERAL ORDER.

The Almighty God, whose Arm is Strength, having of his great Mercy been pleased to crown the exertion of His Majesty's fleet with success, in giving them a complete victory over their enemies, on the 21st inst. and that all Praise and Thanksgiving may be offered up to the Throne of Grace for the great benefits to our country and to mankind:

I have thought proper, that a day should be appointed, of general Humiliation before God, and Thanksgiving for his merciful Goodness, imploring forgiveness of sins, a continuation of his Divine Mercy, and his constant aid to us, in defence of our Country's Liberties and Laws, without which the utmost efforts of man are nought, and direct therefore that

be appointed for this holy purpose.—Given on board the Euryalus, off Cape Trafalgar, Oct. 22d, 1805,

C. COLLINGWOOD.

To the respective Captains and Commanders.

N.B. The fleet having been dispersed by a gale of wind, no day has yet been able to be appointed.

Euryalus, off Cadiz, Oct. 24, 1805.

SIR,—In my letter of the 22d I detailed to you, for the information of my Lords Commissioners of the Admiralty, the proceedings of His Majesty's squadron on the day of action, and that preceding it, since which I have had a continued series of misfortunes, but they are of a kind that hu-

The battle of Trafalgar and the death of Nelson reported in The Leeds Intelligencer, *November 1805.*

Early Victorian fashions, from The Leeds Intelligencer, *April 1840.*

The entrance to Briggate in 1849 (Trinity Church in the background).

Leeds Town Hall as it might have been – a sketch presented with The Leeds Mercury *in 1853, showing the building as it was then planned.*

1853

LEEDS TOWN HALL

problem of crime, particularly in relation to education, or the lack of it, was tackled; but one of the most vexed questions concerned the beer-houses and the 'Casino'.

Kemplay pressed as hard as he could for all amenities that would make life more agreeable. He supported a movement to secure early closing of shops and shorter hours for manual workers. His own great personal campaign was for the abolition, or strict control, of the smoke nuisance: with Dr J. D. Heaton he helped to found a Society for Promoting Public Improvements in Leeds. This Society wished to rid Leeds of the evil reputation it had, and had already held for a full century, of being one of the dirtiest places in the kingdom. The city lacked fine buildings also, and the prospect of a grand new Town Hall excited considerable interest: a great war was waged over the cost, especially for the tower.

From such facts it will be seen that the *Intelligencer* provides a picture of life in Leeds in Victorian times which is unrivalled for its detail. Particularly is this so in three matters: the Church, Poor Law administration, and Town Council proceedings. The last were lively enough, ranging from squabbles about the Waterworks and the Markets to the offence given to one councillor by the borough treasurer's beard. Kemplay took the middle, Conservative, way. He found, as many found, that a price had to be paid for all this social paternalism and that price was bureaucracy and centralization: he took the line that reform should be supported where it was needed, but that well should be left alone.

The Leeds Poor Law Guardians emerge with some honour from a scrutiny of their activities, indeed Farnall, a Government inspector sent to investigate Poor Law administration by them, complained that they treated the old and poor in their care with too much consideration. They told him plainly that they on the spot knew better what was wanted than a remote official in London. As for the Church, this was an era of rapid extension in Leeds, and Kemplay, being a stout Churchman, gave it full publicity. With the dissidence of dissent the editor of the *Intelligencer* had no patience, but then Baines was a Congregationalist; with Roman Catholics Kemplay was equally impatient. Agriculture, as has been said, always had favourable treatment, and the reports on sport, especially cricket, but not forgetting 'knorr and spell', evoke pleasant scenes when they speak of great names.

One revolutionary technical improvement came into use in Kemplay's day. Hardly had the railways superseded the coaches as a means of transmitting news and reduced days to hours, than a new invention reduced the hours to minutes. The electric telegraph was the product of private enterprise, linked with the railways, and was at first neither cheap nor very efficient, but it was of enormous importance for the future. It received a great stimulus from the

Crimean War. The English Electric Telegraph Co., formed in 1846, soon had Leeds upon the first list of its stations and in fact during 1846 and 1847 the city was linked with many places in the North. Obviously it was a link with London that was most urgently required and this was only obtained after irritating delays.

The first important message to reach Leeds from London was received on 23 November 1847: it was a report of the Queen's Speech. Over 130 miles the speech was transmitted within two hours at a rate of 55 letters a minute, or 430 words an hour, so that, as it consisted of 730 words, 120 minutes sufficed, or should have sufficed, to get it whole. But its reception at Leeds was not an unqualified success. The first word was received at 1.5 pm, but the last not till 6.5 pm. The human instruments were very fallible and there were two intermediate stations, at Derby and Normanton, the latter the earliest centre for the North. The telegraph came into regular use during 1848, not superseding the need for the railways at first, but soon making itself indispensable.

Kemplay's was also a great day for advertising, such as it was then. The abolition of the advertisement duty in 1853 encouraged the small advertiser, as charges were now made solely by space occupied. If the advertising of those days did its work effectively, the various households of Leeds must have had their cupboards stocked with a curious assemblage of merchandise: the larders bursting with cordials, syrups, lozenges, and other patent medicines, not forgetting adulterated coffee and cheap tea; the gentlemen's wardrobes stacked with the clothes supplied by Mr Hyam, of Briggate, an extensive and expansive advertiser in the forties, or, later, Mr John Barran's ready-made outfits, especially the 'trousers', whose praises were sung to a startled public, beginning in 1849, in verses of topical interest to suit the season.

The history of Leeds during Kemplay's sway over the *Intelligencer* has not yet been written as it deserves to be written, nor for that matter is there an adequate account of the town during the times of his predecessors. The paper was controlled throughout by Leeds men, though the editors were not always natives of the town. The value of newspapers such as the *Intelligencer* is very great, both to the general historian and the local antiquary: it may be possible to overestimate the value of them as source-material for history, but they provide a corrective to airy generalizations. They show in detail how events affected the lives of our own immediate forebears in a specified place at a specific time and give precise facts. It is these facts that the local historian above all has to assemble diligently. Here he will find plenty.

CHAPTER IV

The now familiar name

[1866–1882]

Christopher Kemplay succeeded in being both witty and wistful in his last spirited editorial from the *Intelligencer* office on Saturday, 30 June 1866. 'Be cheerful, Sir, Our revels now are ended', said the quotation which headed the article in place of a title, and the writer lifted the veil of anonymity by signing his name at the foot of the column. His readers were not unprepared. Step by step he had explained to them how *The Leeds Intelligencer* was to be transformed, its public service increased and its area of circulation widened, as *The Yorkshire Post and Leeds Intelligencer*. Careful of his faithful public to the end, he parted with nostalgic regret from the journal he had helped to build up during twenty-four critical years:

Why should I break through the convenient screen of editorial impersonality, and obtrude myself upon the public, on an occasion which has but a personal and private interest? Why should I lay stress on the fact of my ceasing to publish the *Intelligencer*, and having no longer any part in the management and control of it? The paper itself will continue to be published, though it may be in an altered form, and with its old familiar and distinctive name under partial obscuration. This is what a rational public has to care about, and not about the personal changes that may take place in the publisher's parlour or the editor's room. Yet I think a little good-natured patience will be given me while I express my adieux to the readers of a journal with which I have been intimately connected, and upon which I have almost exclusively occupied my time, for the four and twenty years during which, in that unread corner of the paper at the bottom of the page, my name has appeared, a mark for writs and a pledge to the Attorney-General.

The new venture had given rise to the inevitable gossip, which Kemplay was well able to refute:

... the *Intelligencer*, so far from being a decaying concern, as some were pleased to imagine it, has been prosperous and advancing up to this time, and has been fairly able to hold its own ... As the political organ of the Conservative party in Leeds the

Intelligencer has consistently adhered to the principles it professed, and, I think, it has not ineffectively discharged its functions in this respect . . .

The truth of his observation is borne out by the *Intelligencer's* history. Why, then, the change in policy? Kemplay continued:

This brings me to the circumstances which have led to the developing of the Conservative paper into a daily publication which is to commence on Monday. It was quite natural and reasonable that the party should feel the importance of having a daily organ in the Conservative interest, and the election of last July brought this feeling to a crisis. Without any desire to relinquish my old occupation, I was unwilling to embark on the severe work of a daily publication; but believing, as I most sincerely did, that the expanding of the *Intelligencer* into a daily paper was the best means of accomplishing the desired object with a prospect of success, I consented, when applied to, to treat for the transference of my interest in the paper to a Company which it was proposed to form, and which, I need hardly say, has been formed and is now prepared to commence the daily publication of *The Yorkshire Post and Leeds Intelligencer*.

Kemplay concluded his generous comment upon a note of appraisal for the 'high spirit' in which the Company now entered upon what must be regarded as an 'arduous undertaking'.

On Monday, 2 July 1866, exactly 112 years since the original date when that young and enterprising printer Griffith Wright had begun his bold venture in the first *Leedes Intelligencer*, appeared *The Yorkshire Post and Leeds Intelligencer*, the journal which was the direct growth from his slight four-paged newspaper. Indicating an unbroken sequence since 1754, the paper was numbered consecutively as No.5928. The morning daily was published at the price of one penny, with a Saturday issue containing a Supplement at twopence. The proprietors and publishers were The Yorkshire Conservative Newspaper Company Ltd.

That the *Intelligencer's* transformation into a daily paper was accomplished with no dislocation in service to the public, was a triumph of collaboration between the old management and the new. For ten months the *Intelligencer* had presented its normal undisturbed aspect week by week, while negotiations and preparations were in progress for the daily publication. On 2 October 1865 the Company entered into a preliminary agreement with Christopher Kemplay concerning the purchase 'of the copyright of the Leeds Intelligencer Newspaper, and the good will of his general printing business'. On 7 October a large front page announcement of the Company under a provisional title of 'The Leeds and County Daily Conservative Newspaper Company Ltd' appeared in the *Intelligencer*, outlining the objects of the forthcoming publication and promising that 'the utmost pains will be taken to obtain the best talent to conduct the paper, and an efficient staff to superintend its publication and carry on the business'. Shares were offered for sale to the public, the nominal capital being £50,000 divided into 5,000 shares of £10 each. By the end of the year public eagerness was obviously growing, the share list rapidly filling up, and on 8 February 1866 the first printed draft of the Articles of Association was issued. The name of the Company was now fixed in its present form, but it is extremely interesting to note that at this stage the title of the paper had been decided upon as *The Yorkshire Intelligencer*. The wisdom of thus dropping suddenly the historic and distinctive title may well be doubted, and it is not surprising to find that at an extraordinary General Meeting convened in April this decision was rescinded and the name altered to *The Yorkshire Post and Leeds Intelligencer*; such it remained until 1883 when it became, in response to popular usage, more simply and briefly *The Yorkshire Post*.

On 25 May at a meeting of the directors the Leeds editor and the London editor were formally appointed, with equal status and an initial salary of £550 a year; also the chief assistant editor, who drew £300 a year, and the chief reporter, £200. These appointments were to take effect as from 1 July 1866; the Company's London Office was established at 80 Fleet Street. The original staff numbered, in all, twenty-eight, and the editorial and managerial functions were at first combined.

At the beginning of June began the removal of certain printing materials from 19 Commercial Street to the new headquarters at 8 Change Court, Albion Street, Leeds; and on Saturday, 9 June, Kemplay told his readers that 'yesterday the "Britannia" printing press with which the *Intelligencer* used to be printed before cylindrical printing machines were invented was removed . . . to the new premises in Change -court'. Here in the basement may still be seen an old frail hand-press, an interesting historical link with the past. All this time Kemplay was announcing that in July he would offer for sale 'the whole of the types, machinery, steam-engine, and complete apparatus at present in use for the printing of *The Leeds Intelligencer*'. More powerful and up-to-date machinery was required for the heavier demands and the increased circulation of a daily paper, and to meet this need a new eight-feeder Hoe machine, at that time a considerable advance upon older types, was installed. 'The Directors have provided machinery that will suffice to provide a daily copy of *The Yorkshire Post and Leeds Intelligencer* to well-nigh every Parliamentary elector in the county of York, and they mean to do it', wrote Kemplay. 'They are determined at all events to deserve success', he added, with a note of appraisal for the 'bold and liberal scale' upon which they had 'formed their plant and arranged their establishment'.

The first chairman of a Board of sixteen directors was William Beckett

Denison. Of a distinguished Yorkshire family, he was known and respected by professional and business men in Leeds and the county as an active partner and the real commercial brain of Beckett's Bank – generally known at this time as the 'Old Bank' – whose premises in 1866 were in Lower Briggate. Four years later the bank was removed to Park Row, where it stands today. Although it is now amalgamated with the Westminster Bank, both the historic designations – 'Beckett's Bank' and 'Old Bank' – are to be seen on its portals. During the nineteenth century Beckett's Bank had gradually expanded, weathering the alarming crisis of 1825 and by its great financial stability giving rise to the saying current in Leeds for generations afterwards: 'A Beckett has never failed us yet'. Branches were established at Doncaster in 1868, at Beverley in 1875, and later at Retford and Worksop.

William Beckett Denison was the third son of Edmund Beckett, sixth son of Sir John Beckett, the first baronet, of Meanwood Park near Leeds, who married Mary Wilson, daughter of the learned Dr Christopher Wilson, Bishop of Bristol. Edmund Beckett, who later became fourth baronet, adopted the Denison surname by Royal licence in 1816, two years after his marriage to Maria, daughter of William Beverley, of Beverley, and great grand-niece and heiress of Lady Denison, the widow of Sir Thomas Denison, a judge of the King's Bench. He resumed the Beckett surname upon succeeding to the Beckett baronetcy in 1872, and his example was followed by his eldest son Edmund when he succeeded his father two years later as the fifth baronet. In the year 1886 Sir Edmund Beckett was raised to the peerage with the title of first Baron Grimthorpe, with special remainder to his brother William Beckett Denison, as he was then known. At this time the family resumed the Beckett surname by another Royal licence.

Educated at Rugby and at Trinity College, Cambridge, William Beckett Denison was known as a classical scholar as well as an outstanding figure in the world of commerce. He is described by a contemporary as 'possessing a commanding figure, simple yet gentlemanly in his bearing'. Firm in his adherence to the Church of England, he numbered among his friends the Archbishop of York and the Dean of Westminster; in 1863 he worked actively for the initiation of the Church extension enterprise in Leeds, and as a result of the efforts of the Churchmen of Leeds as much as £140,000 was raised for Church extension in the borough. Living first at Meanwood Park, near Leeds, he took up his residence in 1874 at Nun Appleton House, near Bolton Percy, a beautiful seventeenth-century building.

There was a strong political tradition in the Beckett family, who were loyal members of the Conservative Party and active workers in its behalf. Several of the first baronet's sons and grandsons sat in the House of Commons, and William

Beckett himself represented East Retford from 1876 to 1880, and after 1885 the constituency of Bassetlaw, Nottinghamshire. He is remembered also for his rallying of the Conservative Party in the West Riding during the 'sixties. He showed always a deep interest in the welfare of *The Yorkshire Post and Leeds Intelligencer,* taking an active part in its establishment and continuing to guide its fortunes and its policy. Industrious and careful himself, he appreciated these qualities in others; 'he died in harness', to use the words of his son the Honourable Rupert Beckett, the third member of the Beckett family to succeed in unbroken line to the chairmanship of the Company.

John Ellershaw, the vice-chairman, was also a great Conservative and a strong Churchman. 'Anyone who had anything to do with him in public life', writes a contemporary, 'was sure that he was a perfectly honest man, and what was called a perfectly straight man, never afraid of saying what he thought, never having the fear of man before him, and never pandering for popular applause'. His portrait shows an austere and aquiline face, the monocle adding the final touch of distinction. The house in Change Court, Albion Street, where he was born and which he occupied at this period, adjoined the Company's new offices and some business premises belonging to his father, who was a drysalter and oil merchant. At a later date the Ellershaw property was acquired for the extended offices of *The Yorkshire Post,* and the outlines of the Victorian residence are readily discernible in the gracious dignity of the present main editorial rooms. Other members of this first Board of directors included such eminent Yorkshire personalities as the Honourable George Lascelles, Viscount Nevill, John Musgrave Sagar-Musgrave, and George Taylor: conscientious men of high moral principle and a sense of public duty.

The purpose of the new paper was primarily threefold: to provide a daily organ of expression in Yorkshire, and more particularly in the West Riding, for the formulation of the Conservative Party's basic principles; to link town and country by affording a first-class news service, giving equal prominence to local, metropolitan, and overseas items, with regular sporting reports and literary features; and to counteract the influence of the powerful local contemporary daily, *The Leeds Mercury,* which was regarded as 'increasingly radical' and to be 'outfought'. This paper, which had been in daily publication since October 1861, was noted at this period for its advocacy of Liberalism, its encouragement of the early trade union movement, and its vigorous espousal of the cause of electoral reform upon a basis of manhood suffrage. Its appeal was undoubtedly to the more serious minded and educated section of the middle class electorate, and it gained converts among the upper classes also by the dignity and sobriety of its journalistic standards. It is widely quoted in histories of the industrial

north during the nineteenth century. Most members of the working classes were
as yet too illiterate to be able to appreciate a journal which was as severe in
make-up as all the other leading morning dailies; but in Leeds and other parts
of the industrial West Riding there were the mechanics' institutes and working
men's party organizations, where groups of earnest citizens, anxious to acquire
knowledge on political and social issues, could form readers' clubs and newspaper circles. Here *The Leeds Mercury* exercised great influence. The long reports
of Parliamentary or local speeches and the comments in the leader columns
were especially popular with these genuine enthusiasts. The *Mercury* provided a
challenge which it was necessary to recognize: the more so by reason of the
political contingency of the hour.

At home the year 1866 marked the end of the seven years' Whig-Liberal
ascendancy, first under Lord Palmerston and since October 1865 under Lord
John Russell. At the last General Election the Whig majorities had been heavily
significant in the great industrial centres, notably in Leeds and the West Riding.
Nevertheless, over the country as a whole there was a visible change in the
current of social forces and the alignment of Parties. Disintegration began in the
ranks of the Liberal Party, notably by the revolt of that section of the Liberal
aristocracy led by Robert Lowe and nicknamed by Bright 'the Cave of Adullam'.
At the same time the nucleus of a more radical Party was emerging, although at
this stage diverse and disorganized; but the forces of social unrest had an
energetic and able protagonist in John Bright, whose mass demonstrations in the
provinces are among the most remarkable features of this interesting decade of
history. The position regarding the extension of the franchise was complex and
obscure, involving not only considerations of property qualifications, but also of
an educated electorate. Responsible opinion could not fail to recognize that
social change was on the way, but the cause of manhood suffrage aroused mixed
reactions even among Liberals. In June 1866 a combination of the votes of the
'Cave' Party and of the Conservatives under Disraeli's guidance defeated
Gladstone's Bill on the franchise in Committee, and the Russell Ministry
resigned. The new Conservative Government, formed under the premiership of
Lord Derby, was faced with a political situation of extreme gravity, and laboured under the disability of being in a minority in the House of Commons. Yet the
Party was more compact and better disciplined at this period than were its
opponents; for some twenty years it had enjoyed in the Commons the leadership
of Disraeli, that prophet of genius with his uncanny power of gauging the movement of opinion and his unshakable belief in the dignity and character of the
working man.

Against this national background of complex party evolution and the nascent

William Beckett, M.P., who was the first chairman
of the Yorkshire Conservative Newspaper Company, from 1866 to 1890.
From a painting in the Board Room.

THE YORKSHIRE POST AND LEEDS INTELLIGENCER.

This day is published, at Leeds, the first number of the new daily newspaper, the *Yorkshire Post and Leeds Intelligencer*.

So much of the title as is contained in the words *Leeds Intelligencer* is to be taken to denote that the long-established weekly newspaper of that name is amalgamated with the new Journal.

The political principles of this Journal are Conservative: while supporting every practical improvement, it will resist organic change.

That opinions exist in this country at the present day subversive of that political and social system which distinguishes England from all other nations in the world, no candid observer can deny. That defects still exist in our institutions, which may be amended with benefit to the public, is a truth equally indisputable. By these two guiding facts the political conduct of the *Yorkshire Post* will be regulated. It will be at once Conservative and progressive—a foe to democracy and revolution, but the firm friend of all constitutional Reform.

Those great social questions which in the present age divide, almost equally with politics, the attention of thinking men, the relations between capital and labour, the sanitary improvement of our large towns, the punishment of crime, the reformation of vice, the diffusion of knowledge, and the relief of poverty, will receive that constant and serious consideration which is due not less to their intrinsic importance than to the requirements of those great centres of industry in which the new Journal will be circulated. Arrangements have been made for securing the best and earliest information upon all subjects of interest, both local and general; a full and accurate report of the debates in Parliament, and of the proceedings of all great public meetings; and likewise a constant and authentic supply of Ecclesiastical intelligence.

Especial pains have been taken to ensure the excellence of those columns which are allotted to Monetary and Commercial topics; and upon all that relates to the Markets and the Stock Exchange, both metropolitan and provincial, the *Yorkshire Post* will lay before the public information both exhaustive and precise.

Every kind of National Sport will be reported in the *Yorkshire Post* by writers of ability and experience. Racing, field sports, coursing, cricket, rowing, and athletic amusements in general will be described in detail, and illustrated by original comment. Sports more peculiarly interesting to and articles upon the natural history of the county will appear at intervals from the pen of a distinguished naturalist.

No labour or expense will be spared in bringing out the *Yorkshire Post* as a complete Daily Newspaper, adapted to the tastes and serviceable to the interests of every class of society. Conducted upon these principles...

JOHN L. BOWES AND BRO.'S Monthly Circular

John L. Bowes and Bro.'s Monthly Circular states:—Though a non-speculative article, it has shared in the general depression, and in 15 to 25 per cent. lower in price than in April. Manufacturers and dealers hold small stocks, and, in the face of dear money and the German war, abstain from increasing them. Woollen manufacturers, as a rule, are well employed, particularly for our home trade; but in the worsted branch, which depends in a great degree upon the German market, there is a want of activity.

TRADE REPORTS.

WOOL.

DONCASTER, SATURDAY.—We had rather an increased supply of wool at our market to-day, therefore altogether about 600 sheets on offer—the supply now gradually increasing week by week. The downward movement which has prevailed for several weeks was stopped to-day, and there was a firmer feeling in the trade, which resulted in a quicker sale...

MALTON, SATURDAY.—There has been much more life in the wool trade to-day, and the downward movement has been arrested.

HALIFAX, SATURDAY.—Prices have still a somewhat downward tendency. Notwithstanding the dulness in trade, there was a large attendance of manufacturers...

SOUTH YORKSHIRE COAL TRADE.

More than an average demand for house coal for the Metropolitan market has been experienced during the past week.

IRON AND HARDWARE.

BIRMINGHAM, SATURDAY.—There is less activity in every branch of the iron, hardware, and metal trades...

LINEN.

DUNDEE, FRIDAY. The general market is quiet. Considerable disappointment is felt that no reduction in the Bank rate of discount has taken place...

STOCK EXCHANGE, SATURDAY.

LIVERPOOL COTTON MARKET.—SATURDAY.

Cotton advices have been received this week...

PROVISION MARKETS.

fear of revolution, we read the first statements of aims and policy by the new daily:

The political principles of this journal are Conservative; while supporting every practical improvement, it will resist organic changes. That opinions exist in this country at the present day subversive of that political and social system which distinguishes England from all other nations in the world, no candid observer can deny. That defects still exist in our institutions, which may be amended with benefit to the public, is a truth equally indisputable. By these two guiding facts the political conduct of *The Yorkshire Post and Leeds Intelligencer* will be regulated. It will be at once conservative and progressive, a foe to democracy and revolution, but the firm friend of all constitutional reform. Those great social questions which in the present age divide, almost equally with politics, the attention of thinking men; the relations between capital and labour, the sanitary improvement of our large towns, the punishment of crime, the reformation of vice, the diffusion of knowledge, and the relief of poverty, will receive our constant and serious attention.

'Democracy' (meaning mob rule) is equated, it will be noted, with 'revolution', and it is necessary to see the widespread anti-democratic sentiment in mid nineteenth-century England as arising from no experienced knowledge of the probable effects of a full franchise; and as evoked to some extent by memories of recent mob violence and civil wars abroad, presaging the overthrow of constitutional monarchy for republicanism or the uncertain vagaries of the demagogue. It is hardly necessary to observe that since then the word 'democracy' has changed its connotation in general usage.

This formal announcement of policy had already been distributed as a printed brochure throughout the county, and it appeared at the head of the leader column on each day of the first week of publication. The first leader gave an interesting analysis of the social importance and the widening scope of the provincial Press:

In commencing our new career as a daily journal we feel that responsibilities attach to it unknown to a previous generation. Within the last thirty years a change has been effected in the condition of the English Press, which, important as it is, has been so silently and gradually accomplished that few perhaps have observed its progress. The old line of demarcation between town and country has been broken through. Railways and the electric telegraph have established a frequency of locomotion and a circulation of ideas which rob country society of all that inertness and incuriousness which were once its peculiar characteristics; and the highest questions of politics and literature are discussed with as much knowledge and vivacity in a country town or a secluded manor house as in the smoking room of a London club. A precisely analogous change is visible in journalism. London newspapers have grown less exclusively metropolitan. Country newspapers have grown less exclusively provincial.

The daily newspapers, accordingly, which are now published in the half dozen chief towns of Great Britain are, both in the influence which they exert and the high character which they sustain, something totally distinct from the country newspapers which amused the leisure of our grandfathers; . . . When we consider that the population of two such counties as Lancashire and Yorkshire, to say nothing of the north of England in general, draws now its political opinions quite as much from the Press of Manchester, Liverpool and Leeds as from the Press of London, we shall understand at once the whole extent of the power which, for good or evil, may be wielded by provincial journalism.

This sense of public responsibility has characterized the paper at every stage of its development.

The early numbers were very slender journals, comprising on weekdays two sheets only, giving four pages of seven columns each with closely spaced small type. On some days of the week the front page was devoted exclusively to advertisements and public announcements, but frequently three or four of its columns were occupied by news, often the dispatches from the foreign correspondents of *The Times* or *The Daily Telegraph*. Saturday's issue which carried a supplement of literary articles, book reviews, and music and dramatic criticism, packed its diversity into only four sheets, and works of major importance were reviewed in serial form. To judge these first provincial morning dailies by modern canons of news presentation or literary arrangement would be both erroneous and misleading. Following the example set by *The Times* and other leading London dailies, the make-up was austere and economical of every inch of space. There were no photographs or illustrations of any kind, and very few descriptive headlines. In recent years the *Intelligencer* had adopted the practice of furnishing titles for the leading articles; this custom was now dropped, and the leaders were more closely spaced and prefaced by a summary of news. In the first number this summary, devoid of headings, ranged with remarkable speed and dexterity from the refusal of 'the more Conservative section of the Whigs and the so-called Adullamite party' formally to coalesce with Lord Derby, the latest number of cases in a recent cattle epidemic, the violent deaths of one Ephraim Smith of Halifax and his two daughters, to a tabloid presentation of the latest developments in the foreign wars: in precisely this order. A few months later appeared the headline 'Summary of the News', with the subject matter subdivided into 'Domestic' and 'Foreign'. Headlines varied in size within the narrow limits of 14 pt to 8 pt capitals. Accounts of the continental wars bore headlines reminiscent of the historical text-book, bare and factual; by contrast, reports of railway accidents, which were frequent, had more startling headlines in heavier type, reflecting the horror occasioned by mass deaths nearer home. Regular features varied in position from day to day and from week to week, although the Commercial News was usually on the leader page, giving five closely packed columns to Markets and Trade Reports. Local news received great prominence; and from London came 'Court and Personal' and a column or less of 'Notes from our London Correspondent'. Very popular, from the outset, was the daily letter by 'Observer' on sporting events, which gave detailed guidance on race-meetings, always the Yorkshireman's favourite sport. Reporting was still in most respects tamely discreet, dressed in the stifling garment of Victorian gentility, and meteorological comment confined itself to 'Yesterday's Weather'. There was a column or more of 'Ecclesiastical News' and from the law-courts came full length reports of the outstanding trials of the day. The Imperial Parliament was a daily feature during sessions, with attention devoted to both Houses. A telegraphic summary, occupying often two or more closely printed columns, reported speeches in detail, without interlocution. Speeches in all the chief Parliamentary debates were reproduced verbatim, again without selection or comment and without side-headlines, giving the Parliamentary page a Hansard-like quality. Comment was furnished by the leading articles, which argued the case point by point, often with great complexity.

From its inception the paper was fortunate in the distinctive talent and the conscientious characters of its various editors. The first general editor of *The Yorkshire Post* was John Rowe Kelley Ralph, a man of high academic record and valuable journalistic experience. Of Irish ancestry, he was born at Deal in Kent in January 1824, the eldest son of a schoolmaster, John Ralph. He went up to Oxford in 1845, residing at the Queen's College; from here he matriculated in Easter term of that year. His career at Oxford was distinguished by the honour of election to the presidency of the Oxford Union in succession to the famous Robert Lowe, later Viscount Sherbrooke, and immediately before the future Conservative Prime Minister, Lord Salisbury. He graduated in 1849, receiving the degree of M.A. three years later. In November 1849 he was admitted at Lincoln's Inn and was called to the Bar in 1852. As barrister-at-law he travelled the North Wales and Chester circuit.

At Oxford he had shown persuasive eloquence in public oratory as president of the Union; and the same forensic quality is evidenced in his writing. His literary ability found early expression in a concise and lucid work on the poets laureate, published by Bentley in 1853. The vigorous character he displayed as editor was developed during a period of service with *The Caledonian Mercury*, an independent Edinburgh journal which cradled some brilliant journalists of the age. Immediately before his appointment to *The Yorkshire Post* he was editor of *The Chester Courant,* winning great admiration from his colleagues for his 'high character, honesty of purpose, and purity of motive'.

Contemporaries are unanimous in remarking upon his modest and unassuming disposition; Ralph shrank from putting himself before the public and was known in Leeds by only a limited circle. Nevertheless, he is remembered for his attractive character and for his qualities as a speaker. 'He was the man who was *facile princeps* among after-dinner speakers in Leeds', writes Thomas Wemyss Reid as 'Jackdaw' in *The Leeds Mercury Weekly Supplement* in 1885, 'there was no one at that time who could approach him as a speaker on such occasions, nor do I know that anyone has appeared among us since to rival him. Some of his little speeches will long dwell in the memory of those who had the privilege of hearing them. They were always the speeches of a scholar and a gentleman; but at times they were marked by an eloquence as free from claptrap as it was from anything vulgar.' A devoted member of the Anglican Communion, Ralph's special affiliation in Leeds was with Emmanuel Church, where he served at one period of his life as lay-reader. Always interested in public health services, he was on the Committee of the Hospital for Women and Children. He became a member of the Council of the Leeds Philosophical and Literary Society, where he often lectured with 'great scholarship and critical acumen'.

John Ralph occupied the editorial chair for sixteen years, leaving the paper in 1882; a later appointment as editor of the London *Evening News* took him to the Capital. During his editorship *The Yorkshire Post* gradually developed its high reputation as the great Conservative organ for the county of Yorkshire; and in 1890 *The Sheffield Daily Telegraph* pays a very sincere tribute to the part played by Ralph in this fundamental, if rather unobtrusive, process: 'The foundations for its success had been slowly, laboriously and patiently laid by Mr Ralph'. His distinctive contribution to the character of the paper was of an intellectual quality, which set it upon a firm cultural basis. 'Under his guidance', the Sheffield writer continues, '*The Yorkshire Post* was recognised as a journal which met the requirements of the more cultivated classes of this great county. His leading articles were marked by a fulness of knowledge upon a great variety of subjects, and by a finish of literary style which placed it upon a level of excellence with the best daily papers in London.' This is high praise, but it was merited. The leaders possess often a quality which must be considered brilliant. A selection from them would constitute an entertaining and informative record of the age. Original in thought, incisive in expression, pungent in wit, they show also forceful logic and honest exposition. Notable for objectivity, they escape thus the descent to the abusive, even when criticism is most trenchant.

The paper had its own correspondents in the City, and its special sporting correspondents, from the beginning; but for many news items had to rely upon the agencies – Reuter's, and (after 1870) the Press Association, called into being by the provincial Press during 1868–70. Only *The Times* and the leading London dailies at this period had regular foreign correspondents, and their dispatches were republished by arrangement in the provincial Press. *The Yorkshire Post* had no stop-press column as yet, but in 1870 during the Franco-German War important news items coming through from abroad were printed on galley slips and distributed with the paper. The paper had its private telegraph cable linking the London office with the Leeds, so that news from the Capital came through without delay. By this means the more up-to-date provincial newspapers had a great initial advantage over the Metropolitan Press; but the enterprise of Printing House Square did not suffer it long, and soon the special newspaper trains were rushing the London papers to the provinces to meet the exigent local competition.

The date of *The Yorkshire Post*'s first publication coincided with that of the great Prussian victory over Austria at the Battle of Sadowa, presaging the emergence of Prussian militarism under Bismarck and the struggle for a German hegemony in Europe. The news of the Austrian disaster was reported in the Latest News column, three days later on 5 July, and on Saturday, 7 July, the European situation was analysed in a recondite and masterly leading article
... The Germanic Confederation has fallen to pieces. The apparition of the Holy Roman Empire has vanished from its ruins. A great German monarchy has virtually established itself from the shores of the Baltic and North Sea to the borders of Baden, Wurtemburg and Bavaria. Austria, on the north and on the west, shrinks within contracted frontiers. And Italy is one nation from the Alps to the Adriatic.
Forecasting the movement of the diplomatic pawns upon the chessboard of Europe, the writer saw the high strategic importance of France to the victorious Powers, and concluded with a flash of deep insight:
... But the good fortune of Prussia and Italy is far from being unalloyed, and each in her own way may yet be made to feel that unscrupulous alliances for individual ends are never without their Nemesis, and that there is at least one specimen of the Danai in Europe, who is most of all to be dreaded when he appears as a bringer of gifts.

On Wednesday, 11 July, the front page carried three columns of foreign news, giving the eye-witness account of the battle received by *The Times* from its military correspondent with the Prussian army, together with a report of the repulse of the Garibaldeans at San Antonia on the Tyrolean border on 3 July: the latter from the military correspondent of *The Daily News*. The story of Sadowa was thus spread out over a week; and this leisurely, often rather academic approach to the foreign wars is an eloquent witness to the sense of security and happy isolation enjoyed by Great Britain at the period.

Nearer home were the political battles, notably the popular campaigns on the franchise question which John Bright was conducting at this time in the provinces. His skill and vigour are unquestionable, but he found an opponent worthy of his steel in *The Yorkshire Post*, which continued in issue after issue to explore some of his more fallacious reasoning. In particular, his comments on the noble families of England: 'noble families that I am told came in with the Conqueror', as he said to one of his Leeds audiences, 'and as far as I know it is the only thing they ever did'. Since similar witticisms had been repeated up and down the country, even receiving the attention of a *Times* leader, *The Yorkshire Post* proceeded to explode the ancient legend of the 'Norman intruder' with ingenious counter-wit:

A pure Norman is an impossibility. You might as well look for a descendant of Pericles among the Greek merchants at Manchester . . . The Norman barons of the thirteenth century, for instance, were highly indignant as 'Englishmen' at the intrusion of the foreigners who came in the wake of the Queen of Henry the Third. Nor is this wonderful. The Norman, so far from being a stereotyped character, was one of the most movable of mankind. He became ferociously Papal in Italy; as Scotch as the Scotch in Scotland; more Irish than the Irish in Ireland; and (naturally therefore) a good Englishman like the rest of us here. He was simply a bit of Baltic oak which had been 'French polished' in Normandy.

When Bright visited Leeds on 9 October 1866, the paper contained a full-page verbatim report of his speech, and those of other local Reform leaders, to an assembly on Woodhouse Moor. The most remarkable feature of these occasions was that the public had a general holiday, marched in great processions through the streets of the town, past the Town Hall and up to Woodhouse Moor. On the Moor itself speakers set up their stands, around which groups of political devotees, decorated with ribbons and waving flamboyant banners, declaimed and gesticulated. The degree of Bright's popularity is to be gathered from the report that as soon as he stood up to address them, the crowd rose in a body with loud and prolonged cheers before he had uttered a word to gain their attention. How much of his long and rather diffuse speech was appreciated by this diverse audience is doubtful; but the leader writer noted his comparative silence on the delicate issues of manhood suffrage and vote by ballot: '. . . he never ventured to suggest that Parliament would be improved by the adoption of manhood suffrage. His audience were waiting for some distinct enunciation of his views on the Reform question – some plain and honest admission with reference to the suffrage – but he never got beyond "the sure foundation of the broad and generous representation of the people".'

The constructive views advanced by *The Yorkshire Post* on the franchise at this period, were in favour either of some method of cumulative voting or of the dual vote. It was considered that 'absolute justice to one class may be both absolute and relative injustice of the most overwhelming nature to half a dozen other classes.' As events moved towards the second Reform Bill, designed by Disraeli in accordance with his policy of gradual reform to give a wider vote on the basis of household suffrage, *The Yorkshire Post* guided the electorate in an appreciation of the nature of the proposals. Long tables of statistics were furnished and the wisdom of the extended franchise was thoroughly examined and discussed. The newspaper displayed no narrow partisan spirit, but considered always that to adopt a static conception in the political field was to defeat the very object for which party government was instituted, 'making that an end which was only intended to be a means'. The public was encouraged to do some serious thinking about 'true liberty' and was told plainly that 'a truly free people differs from one which enjoys a fictitious freedom in its voluntary acceptance of certain restraints; not in the abolition of all, nor certainly in subjection to any'. Nor were these mere platitudes, for they have formed the consistent basis of the paper's attitude towards social and political problems throughout its history.

In local affairs *The Yorkshire Post* at this period was a thorn in the flesh to a county borough council which, like most municipal authorities, was showing a desultory and ineffective standard of achievement in face of the urgent problems of public health thrown up by unrestricted building during the accelerated advance of the Industrial Revolution. Following the Disraelian dictum of *sanitas sanitatum, omnia sanitas*, the paper was concerned with the great necessity of improving living conditions in certain areas of the town. That these were intolerable is now common knowledge, and it is not necessary to enlarge upon their squalor. Summer by summer Leeds was stricken by epidemics, smallpox or cholera, but as each epidemic subsided so did public interest in its cause or prevention. It is greatly to the credit of the newspaper that it raised an insistent – even an irritant – voice upon this topic. In one issue a long leading article was devoted to the subject of urban sanitation:

We hear of no active steps taken to inquire into the state of the dwellings of the poor with a view to their remedy. We see the places which were filthy are filthy still; our drains which were choked are choked up still; our close courts and alleys, where the air is stagnant, are stagnating still; the pent-up sewers, teeming with their subtle poisons, are still unventilated. All these tenacious, sleepless ministers of death and misery have their way, and we see no really earnest and far-seeing man among us who can and will lead the way to something better. Let us take the question of water-closets alone. It is now admitted by all first-class sanitary authorities that the diseases of great towns, and cholera in particular, are diminished or prevented by the use of water-closets, and are intensified by the use of a different system. The late experience in the metropolis has put this beyond a doubt. Now let us ask what steps have been taken to introduce water-closets into the dwellings of the poor of this town . . . If we let the day go by, we shall be called to account not for ourselves alone, but for those thousands of our fellow creatures who are now dying daily while we tarry, and for whose lives we shall be held responsible.

It is tempting to linger over the many carefully written articles on social problems appearing at this period; for, true to its first announcement of policy, the paper was a zealous advocate of reform, urging the extended application of the Factory Acts to the smaller factories which contrived to evade protective legislation. In the field of education it made a consistent stand for the provision of general education as 'the foundation of the way of living for the bulk of the community', enriching the lives of the people and providing the best antidote for 'vice, misery and poverty'.

Problems of the Imperial Legislature did not, as yet, awaken much interest in the generality of newspaper readers, but they occupied the attention of many careful and thoughtful students of politics. The journal gave a close and detailed analysis of all important colonial developments. Of these, one of the most vital was the proposed Confederation of the British North American Provinces, and in March 1867 it was discussed point by point in a leader:

It is a matured scheme, the result of thirty years' deliberation in the Colonies which it affects; it has been the subject of long Parliamentary debates in those Colonies, and it is brought before the Legislature of England by delegates, charged with the expression of the settled opinions and convictions of all the representative bodies of their collective countries . . .

The desire of the British North American colonies for responsible government – 'representative constitutionalism', as the leader writer expressed it – was considered in this case 'just and good', and was explained in precise terms:

Ruled, in the first place by a Viceroy, they desire to possess a common Parliamentary representation on the English model, with a permanent Upper House and a Lower Elective Assembly . . . Their Lower House, like that of the United Kingdom, they please to call a House of Commons, which will consist of 181 members.

When, on 1 July 1867, by the British North America Act, the Confederation of the British North American Provinces finally took shape, a warm welcome was given to the newly arisen Dominion of Canada, with its population 'full of intelligence, of energy, of commercial enterprise, of reverence for authority, and of hatred of gratuitous or radical change'.

In Ireland, however, the paper saw a more dangerous situation, because of the recent Fenian outbreaks in that country. Proposals for the Disestablishment of the Church in Ireland were firmly resisted, and suggestions for measures of Home Rule were opposed as premature. On ecclesiastical problems in Great Britain its attitude was free from sectarian bias, but actively in support of the Established Church, eschewing the usual disputes of the time.

The Yorkshire Post was now recognized as the journal which gave the lead to responsible opinion of the north of England. In a time of increasingly prosperous journalism all promised well for the next stage in the paper's development.

CHAPTER V

A wider circle of readers

[1882–1890]

In October 1882, Charles Pebody succeeded John Ralph in the editorial chair. The proprietors had found the ideal man to take over at a period which can be seen in retrospect as a movement out of the old ways of the nineteenth century into the more enterprising methods of a new generation. The Education Act of 1870 was soon to make its impact upon the Press, by providing a wider circle of readers whose appetite often required an easier, more digestible type of journalism. Editors like John Morley and W. T. Stead were already showing themselves awake to the need for brightening their journals by the lighter features which were shortly to work a more general transformation, and their methods were watched carefully by the morning dailies. These innovators of the 'eighties and the 'nineties were highly critical of the heavy overdose of politics which they considered was given to the public day after day, with a corresponding neglect of the wide range of other human interests. They were violently resisted at first by members of the old school of journalists, who feared – and not without cause – the lowering of standards.

Charles Pebody was already well known in the newspaper world as a journalist of outstanding ability. A gifted writer, he had a wealth of original ideas on how to run a paper, and the necessary courage and enterprise to put them into operation. Born in the heart of Warwickshire, at Leamington, he had a love of the country and an understanding of country folk and their tastes which were evident in much of his writing. After his birth, his parents moved to the village of Watford in Leicestershire, where the family had lived for some 300 years. Here Charles Pebody attended the village school, and the schoolmaster was so much impressed by his ability that he undertook his later education privately. The boy's mind thus developed the independence and elasticity which proceed from good individual tuition; and when the days of his formal education were ended, he continued to be a great reader and student of affairs. A friend of the Anglican clergy, he showed an early taste for subjects of ecclesiastical interest. Later, he went up to London and entered a solicitor's office, but his desire was always towards a career in journalism. With this object he learnt shorthand, and began as a member of the body of shorthand reporters who transcribed trials and speeches of the day for the agencies. One of his first reports to attract notice was

Charles Pebody, editor of The Yorkshire Post *from 1882 to 1890.*

of the Cardigan Inquiry into the Balaclava Charge; but it was his rendering of a sermon by Cardinal Wiseman, accepted by the *Morning Advertiser* and generally commended for its style and finish, which drew attention to his unusual talent.

He joined the staff of the *Chelmsford Chronicle*, and at the early age of 21 became editor of the *Barnstaple Times*. He accepted an appointment on the old Exeter

Flying Post of which James Bellerby was proprietor and editor. Asked on one occasion to write a leader on Sir Stafford Northcote's work on financial policy, he performed this task so well that he was made editor of the paper. It is said that this leader, 'full of original thought, brilliant and sparkling', made a sensation at Exeter, and Thomas Latimer, proprietor of *The Western Times*, proclaimed Pebody 'a born journalist'. From Exeter the young man went as

 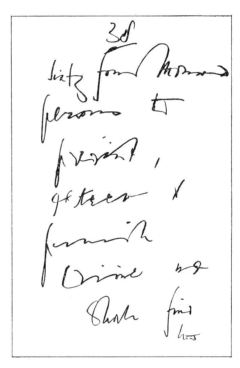

Charles Pebody's handwriting was notorious: only the most experienced compositors could decipher it. The example on the left reads: ' . . . or a fortnight at most which, with the ordinary failures of the day . . .' (the rest is uncertain). The one on the right says: ' . . . sixty-four thousand persons to prevent, detect and punish crime would shortly find . . .'

editor to *The Bristol Times and Mirror*, the chief Conservative organ of the West of England. Here he made a host of friends and wrote often in leading magazines: his articles were in great request, and by this means he supplemented his comparatively slender income. At Bristol in 1875 he won the prize of £50 offered by a Mr James Heywood for an essay on the Athanasian Creed. His masterly little book on *English Journalism and the Men Who Have Made It* was published by Cassell in the year when Pebody entered upon his editorship in Leeds. It shows a first-hand knowledge of the subject and is marked by fluency and lucidity of style.

An extremely friendly man, with a vivacious sense of humour and great generosity of spirit, Charles Pebody was exactly suited to appeal to the generality of the busy and often rather unsophisticated people of the industrial and the agricultural north. *The Yorkshire Post* entered upon a new phase of its history as Pebody set himself the task of making a wider appeal. He found a colleague of his own kind in Tom Charter Sumner – 'Tommy Sumner' as he was affectionately known to his friends in Leeds – who had served the paper since 1866 and had been promoted to the position of commercial manager in 1884.

There were no notable changes in make-up, for in this the lead of *The Times* was still followed, and it was Pebody's avowed aim to make the journal '*The Times* of the North of England'. Until now the paper had made its greatest appeal to the educated reader of the day, and to the student of political, social and imperial problems. It was said to be one of the provincial journals most in demand in the library of the House of Commons, and to have won the commendation of Disraeli himself. Its founders, however, had intended it to be something even more: not so much, as they put it, an organ 'to sustain and confirm political opinions which had already been formed, as to instil those principles in quarters where they did not yet exist'. Further, they were beginning to see a newspaper as, in some sense, 'a popular educator' in this age which was witnessing an extension of the art of reading. For this purpose, they felt, 'it should be widely read, and in order to be widely read it must be, in the generally accepted sense of the term, popular. It must concern itself with the tastes, the pursuits, and the interests of the population.' During the next twenty years this was the steady object of the journal: 'to reflect the genius of the people among whom it circulated, and to represent and identify itself with what was distinctive in the Yorkshire character'.

The contents of the leader columns underwent a perceptible change. No longer were there only one or two complex and closely-knit leading articles, refined and polished to a high standard of literary perfection; but now each day saw three or four leaders, written carefully but in a plainer style. It is possible to discern that they did not all proceed from the same pen; and they dealt with a variety of subjects, designed to appeal to many types of reader. New books sometimes furnished the subject of a leading article, not by way of literary criticism but reflectively, as if to induce further reading on the topic. People were encouraged to look with sympathy upon the hopes and the aspirations of humanity, and while there was no buoyant over confidence in an 'age of progress' the social value of dearly-won reforms was continually empha-sized. In its political attitude, writes a contemporary, the paper at this time took always 'a manly, straightforward view of things and expressed that view with hearty fearlessness. Holding at arm's length the petty personalities of private pique, it has never refused to give a fair blow in the inevitable conflict of opinion.'

Pebody's energy soon made itself felt. A daily 'stop-press' column now announced the edition and contained the latest items of news coming over the telegraph. The notes from London were given the headline 'London Corres-pondence', and the literary page received the designation of 'The Library Table'. Book reviews were still very long as, in general, were the books them-selves. There were elaborate weather charts, showing barometrical readings, with forecasts. Parliamentary proceedings and local political speeches continued to be reported verbatim. An 'Agricultural Review' from a Special Correspon-dent now became a regular feature, while more space was devoted to sporting events – race-meetings, football, cricket, hare-coursing, chess, and billiards. The Commercial News was removed from the leader page to a page in its own right, and the leader page began to wear a more homogeneous aspect. There were still no titles over the leading articles. Foreign news was brightened by main headlines in heavy type, with usually two descriptive cross-heads. Greater attention was paid to the advertisement department, and the rapid increase in this direction soon led to enlargements of the paper's size. By 1884 it comprised eight pages on weekdays, with six columns to a page, and ten pages on Satur-days. Already, since 1870, the annual circulation figures had been growing: 1870 – 4,927, 471 copies; 1871 – 5,007,509; 1872 – 6,559,190; and so on, until 1881 when the numbers had reached 12,802,172, showing an increase of 402,980 on the circulation figures of the previous year. By September 1885 the average circulation was 46,637 daily (the annual computation was dropped at this stage).

Pebody started a paper of miscellaneous features that remained popular for many years, *The Yorkshire Weekly Post*. Here was the valid answer to the inno-vators of the day, and it was at once obvious that the public were ready to find interest in a wide variety of subjects, which made no concessions to 'sensational' tastes. The paper was light, but sound, and bore the stamp of its founder's personality. As 'The Tyke in Mufti', Pebody contributed a weekly article entitled 'Across the Walnuts and Wine', and Tennyson's lines

'After-dinner talk
Across the walnuts and the wine',

appeared regularly as a quotation above the opening paragraph. There was a certain humour in the style of these articles, with a marked tendency to philosophize. 'As one grows older one's faith in sublunary things grows less', remarked the author on one occasion. 'Personally, I could write all that I believe on a very small sheet of notepaper.' Point is given to this piece of hyperbole by the knowledge that Pebody's writing was abnormally large, with long letters sprawling diagonally across the page.

'The Tyke in Mufti' made an immediate appeal. His originality, genuine humour, and crisp style exactly hit the Yorkshire taste. Pebody, it was said, had 'the very happy and rare knack of rendering a dry subject light and entertaining'. He was certainly one who found 'books in the running brooks, sermons in stones, and good in everything'.

In the 'Old Yorkshire Notes and Queries', readers were invited to contribute their own views and questions, with information on topics of local interest, and this feature became extremely popular. There were extracts from literary periodicals, verses, with 'Inconsidered Trifles', a column of humorous stories; and for women readers 'Fashions and Foibles' – a notable venture. 'Homestead and Garden' had also its feminine appeal. There was a Natural History section, conducted by H. Knight Horsfield, the son-in-law of John Ralph. Pebody was the first to recognize the talent of the popular novelist 'Hugh Conway', whose stories he published in serial form in the *Weekly Post*. Among other popular authors whose novels were first published in this way was James S. Borlase, the writer of detective fiction. Halliwell Sutcliffe was a frequent contributor.

For over fifty years *The Yorkshire Weekly Post* was to be a link with home for Yorkshiremen overseas and a budget of news summaries, comments, stories, and features. Under the late Walter Smith, who edited it for 31 years, it reached a high literary standard; but fashions in reading matter changed and in 1929, three years before the celebration of its jubilee, it became an illustrated weekly. Its new editor was John Rintoul Hunt, a specialist in pictorial journalism. In spite of his enterprise it did not attract enough support and was brought to an end in January 1937. Among those who served it as assistant editors were the late R. S. Forman, brother-in-law of the Archibishop of Canterbury, Dr Geoffrey Fisher; Godfrey Talbot, now widely known as a B.B.C. commentator; and H. E. Clapp, who later for a time edited *The Daily Sketch*.

Pebody saw *The Yorkshire Post* prosper in every way. Its growing circulation and extended area of publication inevitably increased its influence. '*The Yorkshire Post* stands now at the head of the provincial Press of the Kingdom', wrote a contemporary in 1890, 'it carries sound constitutional principles into close upon one hundred northern constituencies'. At the General Election of December

1885 it is noteworthy that 'Radical Leeds' (as it had been known) returned three Conservatives out of its five members. How far this success was due to the influence of the paper is not capable of direct proof; but a contemporary political cartoon depicts one of the Conservative candidates resting upon a pillar bearing the inscription 'The Yorkshire Post'.

This period saw some industrial disputes, especially in the coal, iron, and cotton industries. In January 1884, strikes took place at Blackburn, Clitheroe, and other places in north and south-east Lancashire, and many mills were entirely or partly closed. *The Yorkshire Post* deprecated the use of the strike weapon 'from mere desperation', and asked the reason for a reduction in wages on the one hand and a strike on the other:

The Board of Trade Returns and the Revenue Returns all indicate that the general bulk of trade is maintained, if not actually increased; and if prices are not much higher they are not much lower than they have been for several years past. We are at peace with all the world – even with Egypt and the Boers, – and if Ireland be politically disturbed trade there is actually improving at a greater ratio than in England. Why, then, should reductions of wages already enforced in the cotton trade be now followed by a further reduction of five per cent, and the artisan be kept in an impoverished condition? It is a problem, a difficult one, and one openly recognized by the masters.

The remedy, for both sides, was seen in the hope of a Royal Commission to inquire into the causes of the continued depression in the cotton trade.

The great public event of the decade was Queen Victoria's first Jubilee of 21 June 1887. The London Correspondent noted the unprecedented scale of preparation in the capital:

The streets are now more densely crowded than ever, and a complete block of the traffic has resulted in two or three main thoroughfares. The decorations along the route are more complete in character than anything hitherto witnessed. The triumphal arches in St James's Street, the Venetian masts all draped uniformly, the mass of fluttering flags and bannerets making a singularly brilliant spectacle.

In Leeds there was a public holiday, and for Jubilee night an ingenious system of illuminations had been arranged:

At the Town Hall, the centre of the corporate life of the borough, lines of gas jets have been carried from the top to the bottom of the building at both ends of the front of the Hall, and also down the inner sides adjacent to the portico ... But the Clock Tower will be the principal attraction. In addition to being outlined in the same manner as the sides of the building, there is a large crown in gas jets over which are the two letters V.R.

Sixteen thousand gas jets had been installed for this typically Victorian effort; while on Woodhouse Moor an even more dazzling spectacle was provided by 'prismatic lamps, with groups of Japanese lanterns in the centre, and the rockery dotted with fairy lights'. A hundred men were needed to light these lamps and lanterns. But it was all regarded as a great triumph of the century's scientific progress.

To commemorate the Jubilee the journal issued a twelve-page number, bearing a special supplement in the form of an article on 'Queen Victoria and Her Reign', written specially for the paper by Archibald Forbes, famous for his war correspondence in the *Daily News*. There was a long leader on the fifty years of social change, and a shorter one which noted 'the thoroughly English character of the methods in which the Queen's Jubilee is being celebrated'. Pebody had also planned an informative series of articles on the history of Yorkshire during the reign, which were republished later in book form at the very modest price of sixpence, under the title of 'Fifty Years of Progress'. There were no illustrations or drawings, either in the Jubilee number or in the book.

About this time Pebody's health began to fail: he always worked at top pressure; but after a brief illness he recuperated and came back to the office to make plans for an evening paper, with the able assistance of Sumner. In 1888 new offices were constructed, taking in the room where John Ellershaw had been born: the Vice-Chairman himself now became a tenant of the office rooms immediately below, and continued to take an active part in the paper's commercial management. New machinery was ordered, to cope with the increasing circulation and the forthcoming evening issue: six great four-rolled web machines (made by Hoe), each of which could print and fold two four-page, two six-page, and two eight-page papers at the same time. Increases took place in staff, and the *Evening Post* had its separate editorial department from the outset. The first editor, of what was destined to be one of the most successful evening papers in the world, was Alexander Paterson, who introduced the new journal on 1 September 1890, with the words:

The prompt and accurate publication of News – News of all kinds – is the main business of *The Yorkshire Evening Post*.

Impartiality and independence, promptitude and accuracy, are its watchwords – impartiality in recording events and opinions, independence in discussing them, and, as already said, promptitude and accuracy in publishing them.

While, however, the recording of News is its main business, *The Yorkshire Evening Post* will not be dumb. It will discuss events of the day briefly and tersely, frankly and fearlessly. Special features, some of which appear to-day, will mark its columns. But, once more let it be repeated, the aim of the *Evening Post* is to publish the News, and by doing so in a crisp and comprehensive form, and as expeditiously as possible, to place in the hands of Yorkshiremen a first-class evening paper.

At first there were no full-length leaders, but a column of brief comments appeared under the headline 'Notes on News'. A regular feature entitled 'Echoes' was written in the style of the *Weekly Post*'s 'Across the Walnuts and

LEEDS FROM HOLBECK JUNCTION

LEEDS, LOOKING UP PARK ROW.   (REPRODUCED BY COURTESY OF THE ILLUSTRATED LONDON NEWS)

Leeds in 1868: (a) from Holbeck Junction, and (b) looking up Park Row.

Briggate from the railway bridge in 1885.

Wine'. 'Dramatic and Musical Notes' occupied a column; and in the first issue this was devoted to the D'Oyly Carte Opera Company then appearing at the Grand Theatre, and to a Grand Opera Company at the Theatre Royal. A selection of humorous stories bore the title 'Fun and Fancies', and verse was published from time to time. The first to appear were some verses from 'Symphonies' by Cardinal Newman, reprinted from *The Tablet*.

True to its promise to supply frank and fearless discussion, *The Yorkshire Evening Post* did not hesitate to express its views. On the use of the strike weapon by the increasingly powerful trade unions, the paper declared:

These men strike – in itself, under certain circumstances, a perfectly legitimate course of action – but being a law unto themselves, they presume to be a law unto all men. Having struck, they decree that no workmen – whatever their views or circumstances, whether Trade Unionists or non-Unionists – shall take their places. Plain men have a word for this, and it is tyranny.

The correspondence columns were very popular. It was now more than a decade since John Ralph had written his vigorous leaders on sanitary conditions in Leeds, but in 1890 a correspondent is still complaining to the *Evening Post*: 'I am a Liberal; but I am not so much of a partisan as to be blind and dumb when I see the affairs of the Town neglected ... No wonder we want fever hospitals, and new convalescent homes for fever patients, and smallpox hospitals.'

The paper started with four pages and was published at the price of one half-penny; the illustrations were line-blocks and rather amateurish, with the exception of the professional drawings of Harry Furniss, the famous artist. Throughout the years *The Evening Post* has grown in size, first to 6 pages in 1896, later to 8 in 1905; and after the 1914–18 war, 12, 14, and even 16 pages. When it was forty years old, it was said that it was threatened with 20 pages! In 1932 that became a fact, and October 1935 saw a 24-page issue. A 20-page issue, and many 16-page issues, were produced in 1953. The circulation figures show a record of steady expansion: 1932 – 169,327 copies nightly; 1940 – 181,093; and in 1949 the paper had a lead of nearly 100,000 copies nightly over any other evening newspaper in Yorkshire. Today its net sale exceeds 253,000 copies nightly. From the early days of the 1939–45 war until the autumn of 1952 it was produced as a tabloid paper; but with the expansion of business in the post-war years the journal reverted to large page issues, which won appreciation from both advertisers and readers.

The Yorkshire Evening Post has been served by able editors: Alexander Paterson, Alfred Turner, Arthur Grime, Robert Richard Whittaker, Henry Futrell, Barry Horniblow, and Alan Woodward. On 1 September 1950, the journal celebrated its diamond jubilee, quoting the words of its first editor in its first issue, and looking back with justifiable satisfaction across its sixty years of development: 'Its subsequent progress and present ascendancy stand witness to the faith of our founders. On this diamond jubilee day, therefore, we take modest pride in a palpable achievement and pledge ourselves anew to a forward march, consistent with past ideals, but alive to the needs of a momentous and swiftly changing era.'

Charles Pebody did not live to see more than four weeks' production of the evening paper in which he had taken so much interest; the few articles which he contributed to its columns were all by dictation. On 30 October 1890 he died at the early age of 51. His loss was felt in Leeds as a public one, for he had identified himself with the town's cultural and social activities. He had been a member of the School Board, 'taking a spirited part in the debates', he was on the Council of the Literary and Philosophical Society, and a member of the Leeds Library Committee. In the newspaper world he had played a leading part, serving on the Committee of the Newspaper Society, and recently the West Riding Branch of the Institute of Journalists had elected him as its president. A member of the Newspaper Press Fund, he had presided at its recent annual dinner held in Leeds. Only eighteen months previously he had declined an offer of the editorship of *The St James's Gazette,* despite the fact that this would have meant day instead of night work. His heart was in the welfare and progress of *The Yorkshire Post* and its allied papers and before he died he had indicated to the proprietors the person in whom he had seen promise of continuing the line of progress which had already been marked out. He was Henry John Palmer, a man of 37, the able and energetic editor of the *Birmingham Daily Gazette.*

The appointment of Palmer was one of the last official actions on behalf of the Board of directors to be performed by the chairman, William Beckett. In November 1890 he met his tragic accidental death on the railway line near Wimborne. It was a shock to all who had known him, and a great loss to the Company. He was succeeded as chairman by his nephew, Edmund Beckett Faber, who was the eldest son of Charles Wilson Faber, of Northaw, Hertfordshire, and Mary Beckett Faber, the daughter of Sir Edmund Beckett, the fourth baronet, and sister of the first Baron Grimthorpe.

Educated at Eton and at Trinity College, Cambridge, Edmund Beckett Faber became the senior partner in Beckett's Bank. He had been a director of *The Yorkshire Post* since 1881. Maintaining the family's active part in the work of the Conservative Party, he contested the Pudsey Division in Yorkshire in 1900, and from 1901–5 represented the Andover Division in Hampshire. In 1905 he was raised to the peerage as Lord Faber, first Baron of Butterwick. A man of attractive personality and friendly disposition, he exerted a considerable influence upon the fortunes of *The Yorkshire Post*. He continued as chairman until his retirement through ill-health in 1920, controlling and guiding its policy during a critical period. He was an invaluable friend of the new editor who was just entering upon his conscientious and distinguished period of service.

A native of Wotton, near Gloucester, Palmer had been educated at the British School in Gloucester and had served for eight years as an accountant. He had contributed articles to the *Gloucester Mercury* which attracted the notice of Sir William Leng, then editor of the *Sheffield Daily Telegraph*. Leng offered Palmer a post on the editorial staff of the *Telegraph*, where he proved himself not only an able writer, but also a very industrious worker in the exacting routine duties of his position. His habit of methodical tabulation of figures and his unwearying pursuit of detail made him especially valuable for the drawing up of broadsheets of a political character; he was a welcome recruit to the Conservative Party in Sheffield. After eight years with Leng he was said to be 'his right hand man', and he passed from the assistant editorship of the *Telegraph* to assume editorial control of the *Birmingham Daily Gazette*.

CHAPTER VI

The old school and the new

[1890-1903]

Palmer found great scope for his talents upon his appointment as editor of *The Yorkshire Post*. He watched carefully over the progress of all three papers issued from the office, exhibiting a comprehensive grasp of the diverse problems connected with what had now become a large and important business undertaking. Outside, he was equally active. He became president of the Newspaper Society and of the Institute of Journalists, and even found time to fulfil the duties of a justice of the peace, being 'most assiduous in his attendance at the Town Hall'. A close friend of the Bishop of Ripon, the eloquent Dr Boyd Carpenter, he took a great interest in Church affairs and from time to time read papers on topical questions before the Ripon Diocesan Council.

The *Manchester Guardian* portrayed the new editor as 'a born journalist and especially a born editor. His mind was intensely practical and instant in the decision, and he had a free and vigorous style of writing which encouraged friends without inflaming opponents. No man ever had a more insatiable hunger for work. He was the real head of his journal, and all its nerves met in his brain . . . To him the control of a great newspaper was a kind of religious trust, and his strong faith in his own aims gave him a courage which is not common.' With his staff he earned the reputation of a strict disciplinarian, being particularly severe against any 'journalistic sin for which the only excuse was indolence or carelessness'. This severity was matched by a reserve of manner which was often misunderstood; only those who succeeded in penetrating his reserve discovered the rare qualities of character which his aloofness seemed to mask.

A contemporary has left an interesting picture of this editor at work:

He was accustomed on most days to put in an appearance at the office at four o'clock in the afternoon, and after attending to departmental work he would spend a considerable time with his secretary in dealing with correspondence. At half past seven o'clock he returned home for dinner, but at nine he was again at his post and usually remained there until three or four o'clock in the morning, personally revising various editions of the paper as they were struck off the press. Mr. Palmer's work in the editorial columns was invariably distinctive . . .

Palmer, however, was not primarily 'a writing editor', preferring to direct and organize, but it was said that 'an article or a note from his pen in the columns of the morning journal could be readily detected by many readers who were inclined to speculate on their knowledge of literary style'. 'That's Palmer', people would exclaim as some forceful phrase arrested their attention. Casting a sidelong glance at his high journalistic standards, W. T. Stead described him as 'a journalistic Bishop whose diocese is Yorkshire and the whole north of England'.

Like Pebody, Palmer was progressive in his outlook and refused to be bound by tradition as such. 'He was for ever improving his paper, and believed in being up to date. He flung aside the worn-out garments of a jaded journalism and dressed up his columns in the fashion of the day, but always with this proviso, that they remained seemly. He believed in the dignity of the Press'; so wrote the *Sheffield Daily Telegraph*, noting also that 'he had little sympathy with the new journalism of the cheaply sensational kind, yet, in many respects, he was a new journalist'. An article which he contributed to *The Nineteenth Century* on 'The March of the Advertiser' was directed against the new methods of advertising which used 'deft subtlety of arrangement' so as to mislead the public. 'The danger which threatens the well-won glory of the Press in this country', he wrote, 'is not bribery in any direct sense, but bribery by advertisement'. In a talk to West Riding journalists on 'The Old Journalism and the New', his conclusion was that the new journalism in its best sense was immeasurably superior to the old; but it had 'outgrowths, excrescences, and conditions' of which he could not approve, and there were some features of the old which he hoped would always be retained. He became famous in the north of England for his firm opinion that 'journalism always had, and always will have, what the clergy sometimes call "a preaching order"'. No man ever laboured more strenuously than he to place his journal upon a strong managerial and commercial basis; and none ever insisted more forcefully that this, in itself, was essentially a means rather than an end. 'I would rather see newspaper proprietors suffering from their fidelity to newspaper ideals', he declared, 'than that their properties should be handed over to the dividend hunters, who care only for a return for their money, and would say "To Jericho with all your high traditions", for, when it is too late, they will find out, after all, that fidelity to the public interest lay at the root of their prosperity'. A newspaper was a transcendent influence upon the lives of others, and it was Palmer's constant effort 'to write nothing and to say nothing that was not for the good of his fellow-men'.

In improving the make-up of the morning paper, Palmer paid special attention to headlines, which became more numerous and extremely terse and descriptive. The size of page was enlarged to carry eight columns, and by the end of the century the journal comprised ten pages as a daily average, with twelve pages on Saturdays; the advertisement section began to develop, and larger advertisements made their appearance at this stage. 'News of the North' was featured daily, and from the London Correspondent came 'Notes on Current Topics'. There were usually four leaders, without titles; they were preceded by the Summary of the News in the old style. Palmer was responsible for a great development in the correspondence columns of the paper, which were given special prominence and more space. The editor's efforts were all for his public, and his reward was their increasing interest and the extension of the journal's influence far beyond the boundaries of Yorkshire, to the borders of Cumberland, Northumberland, and Lancashire. In the words of G. D. Faber, a member of the directorate, to the York Conservative Association, 'he considered the editorship of a great paper a great public trust, and one not to be lightly used, not to be used solely and merely for party purposes, but as a great instrument for the education of the community'. In all this, Palmer was building for the future.

This period saw the birth of the Independent Labour Party, and on 14 January 1893 its first Conference was opened at Bradford, under the leadership of Keir Hardie. There were 150 delegates from various parts of the country, and the speeches received verbatim reports in eight columns of *The Yorkshire Post*, with vigorous comment in a leading article. Keir Hardie had spoken of 'the waiting voiceless millions whom they specially represented, looking longingly and hopefully to the Bradford Conference', a remark which the editor considered inapplicable to the country's social development:

. . . at least it may be said that by means of the franchise, and of national education, and of trade unionism, they have been encouraged to find voices and choose for themselves their representatives . . . The truth is that the masses in this country are devoted to practice rather than to theory; give them good laws and sound administration, and they do not care whether their representatives in Parliament are squires, or barristers, or merchants, or market stall-keepers, or artisans, or 'unemployed'. They do, as a rule, care for the moral and social qualities of their representatives.

But the leader writer was not entirely hostile, noting that some parts of Keir Hardie's programme had long been advocated by Conservatives and opposed by the Liberal Party on the 'purely partisan' principles of the *laisser faire* economy which continued to obstruct social improvements. 'It is impossible for any man to keep his eyes open as he walks through the streets of any of our large towns and to praise this as the best of all possible worlds.' Nevertheless, the paper pointed out that the formation of a separate Party by 'the advocates of Socialism' was inevitable, in view of the latter's desire to carry industrial legislation further than the Conservative Party was willing to go:

Manufacturing and distributive co-operation, carried on side by side with individual-istic enterprises, must be harmless when they are not absolutely good; and if they fail, their rivals are still in existence. Private enterprise has often been proved to be more advantageous than Socialism in Great Britain; it has created industries, as Socialism has not . . .

The words have lost none of their controversial force today.

During the great dispute between the miners and the colliery owners con-cerning the Federated Unions' campaign for an Eight Hours Act, *The Yorkshire Post* feared that as a nation we were in some danger of 'going too far in our revolt against excessive labour', pointing out that 'any man in any age who has won prizes of importance to his fellows has never counted his hours of labour'. Granting the highly accelerated rate of labour brought about by the introduc-tion of machinery, it was feared that this benefit might be offset by a gradual reduction of hours worked. In the coal strike of 1893 the paper continued to take this attitude, but launched a public appeal for the benefit of the families of miners who were affected by the strike, with the result that contributions amounting to several thousands of pounds were received. Some years later, during a general appeal for the widows and children of the sixty men who lost their lives in the Micklefield Colliery disaster, over half of the £80,000 given by the public was received through the channel of the Editor's appeal, in support of which Queen Victoria sent a donation of £50.

Much attention was devoted to ecclesiastical problems of the day, and it was the journal's openly avowed policy that the Press must not be harnessed to schools of thought which might 'inspire it with a partisan zeal'. There must be a profound reverence for religious truth, accompanied by a capacity 'to look at religion whole, and not in its segregated divisions'. On the more practical social problem of clergy incomes in the Church of England, the paper's comments anticipated the developments of more than half a century, and contended for the maintenance of a high level of recruitment:

Our clergy must devote themselves with singleness to the work whereunto they have been called; and to lower them socially and intellectually would be to revive some of the darker pages in the ecclesiastical history of the country.

Opposing the idea that the clergy should pursue some secular employment in order to supplement their diminishing incomes, the paper thought that the remedy was obvious:

It is clear that the laity will have to come to the aid of the clergy more freely than they do . . . The poverty revealed is no shame to those who endure it; it is a shame to the wealthier members of the Church of England.

Great progress was made at this time in the publication of foreign news, and in the South African War which occupied the years 1899–1902 *The Yorkshire Post,* in conjunction with other leading provincial newspapers, formed syndicates to secure war telegrams and the services of correspondents in the battle zones; in many cases arrangements were made for the simultaneous publication of the letters and telegrams received by leading London journals. News items, reports from correspondents, and editorial comment were now synchronized; elaborate plans were drawn up for the guidance of readers during outstanding events such as the Defence of Ladysmith, and reports of the fighting carried column head-lines in large heavy capitals, with similarly heavy cross-heads. On the war itself and on the history of the Boer Republic, the editorial department wrote a series of articles for the morning journal which was so highly valued as to necessitate its republication in a single volume.

Before the war was in sight of an ending Queen Victoria died, on Tuesday, 22 January 1901, at 6.30 in the evening. 'It was exactly seven o'clock when the momentous news was received in Leeds', announced *The Yorkshire Post* next morning. 'Within a few minutes a special edition of *The Yorkshire Evening Post* was circulating the intelligence through the streets, the hotels, and the clubs, and it was not long ere the residents in the suburbs became aware of the all-important event.'

On Monday and Tuesday of that week twelve-page issues of the morning paper had given the public full news bulletins of the Queen's illness, and on Wednesday, the 23rd, a twelve-page issue with black-bordered pages announced in large two-tier column headlines: 'Death of The Queen. A Peaceful End Last Evening.' The country was in a mood of tense emotion, and to this mood the leader writer addressed his comment: 'Our effort today should be to realize that we are passing through one of the great moments of history . . . The duty which the privilege of having served under the direct sway of the great Queen lays upon us is that of carrying forward with reverent steadfastness the traditions which she created and by which she ruled.' The news from London was given a new headline as 'Notes and Comments', from our London Correspondent (which continued to be the descriptive title until 1920). A special article, unsigned, on 'The Mission of Queen Victoria', was written in a simple and telling style, with such cross-heads as 'A pattern of Womanhood', 'The Sceptre in a Firm Hand', and in the centre of the page was inset an engraved drawing from a portrait of Queen Victoria. There were also 'Yorkshire Memories of the Queen' and 'Some Personal Notes', by 'one who enjoyed special opportunities of observing her'.

Lord Faber, chairman of the Company from 1890 to 1920.

LEFT: *H. J. Palmer, editor of* The Yorkshire Post *from 1890 to 1903.*

BOTTOM LEFT: *J. S. R. Phillips, editor of* The Yorkshire Post *from 1903 to 1919.*

(REPRODUCED BY COURTESY OF LEEDS PUBLIC LIBRARIES)

BOTTOM RIGHT: *Arthur Mann, C.H., editor of* The Yorkshire Post *from 1920 to 1939.*

THE EDITOR WHO FOUGHT APPEASEMENT

W. Leighton, news editor of The Yorkshire Post
from 1900 to 1912.

*J. E. Thornton, general manager of the Company
from 1904 to 1923.*

James Sykes, chief assistant editor to J. S. R. Phillips.

*Tom Charter Sumner, commercial manager of the Company
from 1884 to 1904.*

The Hon. Rupert Beckett, chairman of the Company from 1920 to 1950.
From a portrait by Henry Carr.

On Saturday, 2 February 1901 appeared another black-bordered issue with many drawings, together with the descriptive article 'Across the Solent', which related in graphic prose the story of the historic voyage of the Royal yacht *Alberta* from Cowes to Portsmouth, bearing the mortal remains of the late Queen. The author of this famous article was John Foster Fraser (afterwards knighted), the special correspondent of *The Yorkshire Post* at this time, whose trip 'round the world on wheels' with two other cycling enthusiasts had won admiration in the 'nineties. Two days later another twelve-page, black-bordered paper was published, and a second article 'Last Scene of All', by John Foster Fraser, described the ceremony in St George's Chapel. So widely appreciated were Foster Fraser's articles that they were republished in pamphlet form, illustrated by sketches – four full-page illustrations and a medallion portrait of the late Queen.

In the following year Palmer's untiring devotion to duty began to take its physical toll, and his last months with *The Yorkshire Post* were clouded by ill-health. He died in February 1903 at the early age of 49: but into this short span of life he had crowded much achievement. His death was mourned in Yorkshire and throughout the north of England; and his name is forever remembered in the annals of journalistic history as one of the great editors. At the funeral ceremony the Bishop of Ripon spoke with deep feeling and reverence of a man whom he respected as a writer and loved as a friend. Taking the significant text of Romans, xiv, 7: 'For none of us liveth to himself, and no man dieth to himself', Dr Carpenter reminded his listeners of the supreme importance to the community of the responsible work performed by editors of great newspapers:

Often ill in health, tired with the strain of long-continued work, they have to produce the views which are presented to the public every morning and still hold true the balance of scrupulous honesty and accuracy, of righteousness and reserve. All honour to such men who hold the scales of life still level, and endeavour to preserve in our home life, in our politics, and in our national life, the great laws of righteousness. The power of lives such as Mr Palmer's lies surely in this, that they hand to those who follow a torch which burns clearly and brightly, without any of the smoke of that which is degrading, vicious, and polluting. We have lost one who conducted a paper which made for righteousness.

CHAPTER VII

'Twixt Trent and Tweed

[1903–1919]

Palmer's standard of editorial achievement was maintained and enhanced by his successor, one of *The Yorkshire Post*'s greatest and most attractive personalities, whose warm humanity, joyous spirit, and literary excellence are stressed in many sincere tributes to his memory. Noted by Palmer for his distinctive editorship of *The Manchester Examiner*, Phillips had been invited in 1891 to come to Leeds and serve as chief assistant editor and leader writer. To work under Palmer was regarded as a valuable opportunity in the world of journalism, and Phillips accepted the offer. He was virtually editor during the last months of Palmer's illness, and in 1903 Edmund Beckett Faber (later Lord Faber), on behalf of the Board of directors, raised John Searle Ragland Phillips to the editorial chair.

Born at Pendleton, Manchester, in 1850, John Phillips was of Welsh ancestry with a strain of the Norseman in his blood: it was manifested in his fine physique, fair hair, and ruddy complexion, as also in his love for the sea and foreign travel. His father, an accountant, died when John was very young; and his mother, in partnership with an aunt, set up a boarding school at which he was educated until the age of 11. After further years at a private school the boy worked in a Manchester wholesale drapery warehouse. His leisure was entirely devoted to a process of self-education which bore rare fruit. During the lunch hour he read in the Manchester Public Reference Library, and in the evenings attended classes at Owens College, where he specialized in political economy and in English language, history, and literature: the last two subjects he studied under Dr (later Sir) A. W. Ward, who became his life-long friend and at whose invitation he contributed his article on the growth of British journalism to the *Cambridge History of English Literature*. One of the first members of the Manchester Shakespeare Society, Phillips succeeded Professor C. H. Herford as its secretary. At Owens College he won many prizes and contributed prose work and verse to the college magazine. In this way, working by day in the Manchester warehouse and studying and writing in his spare time, he spent his early youth, and he was already married and 27 years of age when he entered upon the journalistic profession in which he was to win great distinction.

John Phillips began his career as sub-editor of the old *Kendal Mercury*, which was absorbed by a rival paper at the end of his first year of service. Later appointments took him to Gateshead and to Worcester; he came north again to serve as chief sub-editor, first of *The York Herald* and then of *The Newcastle Leader*. A warm supporter of the Unionist cause during the Home Rule division of 1886, he found scope for expression on joining the editorial staff of *The Scotsman* as leader writer. Here he showed also that capacity for book reviewing which distinguished his later editorial career. Appreciative of his services, the Liberal Unionists in 1889 asked him to accept the position of editor of *The Manchester Examiner*, which they had just taken over. When, two years later, this paper was discontinued John Phillips joined the staff of *The Yorkshire Post*.

Alike in editorial ability and vigour of mental outlook, Palmer and the newcomer were nevertheless contrasts in temperament. Palmer's austerity had often chilled his staff, who were wont to regard him with awe and to approach him with diffidence. Phillips now broke down this barrier, reminding those who worked with him that although there must be authority, with finality in editorial decisions, this need not be over-emphasized. All, he said, 'from the editor down to the "printer's devil" were colleagues, with no question of rank or class'. He taught each individual to see himself as part of a whole, engaged in a wonderful creative work. He taught also the true dignity of the labour, for a man might be 'only a cog in a machine; but it was a big machine, and it would not work so smoothly unless his work were well done. Therefore he was proud of it'; so wrote one who appreciated the new editor's attitude. He was Alexander B. Bell, the assistant editor of *The Yorkshire Evening Post* after 1912, under Arthur Grime, the *Evening Post* editor who later became general manager. Bell illustrates further with a personal reminiscence: 'I was on my way home from the office one afternoon when I met Mr Phillips on his way to it. Almost automatically I raised my hat. I was surprised a minute later by Mr Phillips running back to me and saying: "Mr Bell, when you meet me, please don't raise your hat. Remember we're colleagues" . . . I can never forget the emphasis on that word *colleagues*.'

With the directorate Phillips's relations were particularly happy, and of the many stories told about him and Lord Faber, the popular chairman, perhaps the most typical is that of a 'friendly wrangle' between them about a pig which, said Lord Faber, Mr Phillips had promised to let him have. 'Phillips vowed that

Lord Faber had got the pig, while Lord Faber maintained that he had only received half a pig', says the raconteur, 'but what were the rights and wrongs of the question I never learned, for it only came out as a bit of chaff received with uproarious laughter at an office social gathering.'

In 1904 the paper lost its competent commercial manager, Tom Charter Sumner, who died in March, in his fifty-ninth year. Sumner, it has been noted, was one of the few survivors of that small band of workers who had produced the first copy of *The Yorkshire Post and Leeds Intelligencer* nearly thirty-eight years before. Devoted to duty and friendly towards his fellow men, Sumner had won a high reputation by the consideration he showed always for those who worked under him. At the Company's Annual Meeting held only a few weeks previously, the chairman had told shareholders: 'that there was no one upon whose opinion concerning the general commercial position of the paper the directors more relied'. His name had figured in the publisher's imprint of *The Yorkshire Post* for nearly thirty-six years, and for the last twenty years he had been commercial manager of the morning paper.

Sumner was succeeded as general manager by Joseph Edward Thornton, who had joined the staff in 1872, and was already serving as commercial manager of *The Yorkshire Evening Post*. He proved a capable and energetic organizer, at a period when provincial newspapers were faced with increasing competition from the London Press. Under Thornton's management came important developments in newspaper methods. Half-tone blocks were brought into general use and process engraving plants were introduced; production in general was considerably accelerated after 1905. Methods of delivery were also improved, and from this date the horse and trap, which had been used previously, was gradually superseded by the motor car. Within a few years delivery of newspapers was carried out entirely by motor cars. To Joseph Thornton belongs the credit of having blazoned the famous alliterative sign ''Twixt Trent and Tweed' on large yellow boards throughout the north of England: before his advent as general manager the advertisement caption at the head of the paper was: 'The leading journal from the Trent to the Tweed'; it was soon transformed into 'The leading journal "'twixt Trent and Tweed"'. At this important period of development Mr Thornton had a useful colleague in his private secretary, Mr Ernest Osborn, who, it will be seen, was destined to play a great part in the history of the paper, and who is now general manager and a director of the Company.

The news editor of *The Yorkshire Post* when Thornton became general manager was William Leighton, a man of 56, who occupied this position of increasing responsibility until 1912. Public interest in news of all kinds was growing, and in particular there was a quickened interest in foreign affairs. At the same time, desire for what Alfred Harmsworth termed 'human interest' items had increased. The selection of news, in face of the growing competition from papers catering only for popular tastes, demanded a nice sense of balance and sound judgement. Movements associated with the business life of the north of England, with the country's trade in general, with Parliamentary procedure and with imperial developments, continued to be reported at increased length as the paper increased in size. Leighton gave especial satisfaction to the agricultural community in the north of England at this period, knowing exactly the secret of how to interest farmers and farm workers. He was an expert on the subject, and for some twenty years he wrote the 'Annual Review of Agriculture' for the *Journal of the Yorkshire Agricultural Society*.

Phillips's chief assistant editor was James Sykes, of whom it was said that 'he was a journalist who had been "through the mill" as the phrase goes, and knew his job from A to Z. His election to the presidency of the Institute of Journalists was a well-deserved honour.' His methods were meticulous and methodical, and he had his own private collection of Blue Books and official publications in his room. A quiet, unassuming man, with no trace of self-importance in his bearing, he was nevertheless imbued with that degree of self-confidence necessary for his task and could assume responsibility without fear. Edmund Phillips, the editor's son who helped his father and later served as chief assistant editor under his successor, had his father's warm friendliness of disposition. It was a good trio, and the editorial columns were marked by an abundance of knowledge on subjects of diverse interest, while in the politics of the day the paper exercised a steadying effect on public opinion.

Another personality who served at this period calls for mention because of his long association with the paper and his public reputation. Herbert Thompson, whose contributions appeared over the initials H. T., was a distinguished critic in music and art. The son of a Leeds bank manager, he was educated at Wiesbaden, where he acquired special knowledge of German music, and at Cambridge. A barrister-at-law, he had little taste for legal practice and in 1886 he began his long association with *The Yorkshire Post* as music and art critic and served under four editors. His successor as art critic writes: 'He won a reputation for not tolerating slovenly work or inferior music. He undoubtedly did a great deal for musical appreciation in the north by his lucid and sympathetic interpretation of the Masters.' His fine head of silver hair, fresh colour, and classic profile made him a much-remarked figure at concerts. In recognition of the stimulus he had given to the intellectual and cultural life of the north by his well-informed and scrupulous opinion and readiness to welcome new departures in the arts, the University of Leeds conferred upon him in 1924 the honorary degree of Doctor of Letters. His work had great encouragement from Phillips, who was always known as a man of letters and a man of affairs in equal degree. In 1904 a regular column under the heading Music and Art appeared in *The Yorkshire Post*. It gave sound and lucid comment and brought critical acumen to bear on serious works.

In the realm of sport also one name at least must be recalled. 'Old Ebor' (A. W. Pullin), who joined the staff in 1889, served as a sports writer under three editors and contributed both to the morning and evening journals. He wrote with fine integrity and deep knowledge on cricket and rugby football, saw the golden age of the summer game when 'Ranji', Trumper, F. S. Jackson, Hirst, and Hobbs were at their best, and died in 1934 on his way to a cricket match. He is remembered not only as one of the most authoritative commentators of his day on two sports, but for his *History of Yorkshire Cricket, 1903 to 1923*.

The editorial columns of *The Yorkshire Post* at this period were richly distinctive and attracted attention throughout the country. Phillips himself was preeminently 'a writing editor', and he contributed many leading articles to the paper. Often the editor did not begin to write his own leader until nearly midnight. One who worked with him has left some notes of his daily timetable: a day's extract serves to illustrate his capacity for sustained exertion:

Thursday – Attended with a deputation at the Board of Trade, 12.30, and made a speech of half-an-hour; back in the office at Leeds at 6 pm; went to supper at 10 o'clock, returning at 11.30, wrote or dictated leader, and remained at the office until about 4 am on Friday.

His articles were notable for their literary quality and lucidity of thought. They have provided models for many young journalists. He saw events against a wide background, and, says a colleague: 'when he wrote the first leader, he had difficulty in keeping it from spreading to two columns; and whatever its immediate subject might be, you could generally rely upon its taking the whole world for its province before it was done'.

J. S. R. Phillips brought to his work encyclopaedic knowledge and a quick and retentive memory. On literary topics he had an abundance of quotations. Asked on one occasion how he 'came to know all these things', he replied in a witty paradox: 'When I was a young man I wasted my time in acquiring an immense amount of useless knowledge, which I have found to be of the utmost value in later days!' During the First World War he produced a series of brilliant leading articles showing great knowledge of military strategy. He told newspaper readers, who wondered that a civilian editor should have the technical knowledge of a soldier, that during the Franco-German War in 1870 he had been deeply interested in military history from the viewpoint of tactics and campaigns, and had read many books on the art and science of war. In other spheres he was equally learned: 'with the soldier he could talk war, with the farmer agriculture, with the parson theology, with the sculptor and painter he could discuss art; he was equally at home with the university professor or leader of industry. Truly he could say *Homo sum; humani nil a me alienum puto*.'

During his editorial direction, the paper's 'steadying influence' in a period which saw much social and industrial unrest was greatly appreciated, and leaders of the Labour Party in Leeds valued his open-minded, fair, and tolerant attitude.

Phillips could take an independent stand, on occasion, even when his opinions ran counter to certain currents of feeling in his own Party. *The Yorkshire Post* won national repute within a few months of his accession to the editorship for its balanced attitude on free trade in the great fiscal crisis which followed the Budget of 1903, during the Premiership of A. J. Balfour. When C. T. Ritchie, the Chancellor of the Exchequer, proposed to balance his reduction of direct taxation (in the fourpence taken off the income-tax) by dropping the corn-duty for the benefit of the indirect taxpayer, there was a serious split in the Cabinet, and the whole question of tariff reform was raised. Austen Chamberlain, the Colonial Secretary, who was anxious to draw the Mother Country and the Dominions into a closer economic union against imports from foreign countries, forced the issue on 15 May by his Birmingham speech in favour of Imperial preference and fiscal retaliation against foreign tariffs. The dispute dragged on through the summer of 1903, and in September, Austen Chamberlain resigned; as did also four free trade members of the Cabinet, including the Duke of Devonshire. In an attempt to avert the crisis, A. J. Balfour put forward a proposal of his own in a pamphlet entitled *Economic Notes on Insular Free Trade* which suggested that the Government should be given power to try to counteract the adverse influence of certain foreign tariffs by means of retaliatory duties. Its moderation pleased neither party in the dispute.

The Yorkshire Post fought long and vigorously for free trade, now and later, but recognized the spirit which animated the Government's proposals. Believing always in the fundamental value of free trade, the paper gave its measured approval to a 'temporary departure from the system of allowing trade to take its natural course', and commented:

This departure is justified; provided always that we do not inflict more injury upon ourselves in the process than was caused by the restraint we desired to remove. This is the policy of Mr Balfour and of the Conservative Party, and as a policy it is unaffected by the remarkable expansion of our trade that has taken place under existing conditions. This may have rendered the application of it less urgent than would have been the case with a declining export trade, but the principle is indisputable ...

Similarly, during 1909–10 the land taxation proposals of the Lloyd George Budget were examined with great ability in the leader columns and much interest was displayed by readers. The editor appended some long and acutely reasoned notes to letters from supporters of the land taxes, and these were often used to advantage by Mr Lloyd George's leading opponents. The paper's sustained opposition to the granting of votes to women was famous, and many saw in it a reflection of the editor's known distaste for the employment of women in a professional or a public capacity, and for the idea of women politicians in particular. However, the discussion was in fact conducted on a higher level than that of a personal opinion. Mr Phillips saw clearly from the outset that, once the vote was conceded, its application would have wide repercussions.

On foreign affairs the paper provided an efficient news service, with the type of knowledgeable military comment to which reference has already been made. Provincial newspapers were making notable advances in a field where they had once been behind the leading London dailies, and during the war in the Far East in 1904 *The Yorkshire Post* secured the services of 'a large number of correspondents, moving with the campaigns or stationed in various centres of information in the Far East'. Maps and plans were given for the geographical and military guidance of readers.

The outstanding aspect of the paper's attitude to foreign affairs during the years which led up to the First World War was its continual emphasis upon the value of the British Navy. Not only in the Far East, but also in Europe the portents were unfriendly, and Germany presented an inscrutable demeanour. Phillips was known for his sympathy towards Germany and his anxiety to promote friendly relations between that nation and ourselves. But he was always a realist and editorials warned readers that 'if there were to be a war it would be made on the same plan as that of 1870, and with the same purpose ... Bismarck did not hesitate to falsify a telegram in order to keep the flame alight and precipitate the conflict on which he had determined.' Noting 'the subtlety of German diplomacy', the paper stressed the importance of British sea power which could pave the North Sea with ships. 'We question very much', said a leading article, 'whether Germany would venture upon war did she know that the British Fleet would support the armies of France.'

At the same time, many leading articles showed that it was at once this country's interest and her duty to attempt to be on terms of complete friendship with Germany. In science, in the arts, in literature, and in industrial invention, no less than in trade, the two nations had mutual relations which could be of inestimable benefit to both. In 1907 the editor was one of a party of British journalists who visited Germany in order to promote better feeling between the two countries. At Potsdam, the Kaiser asked that a provincial journalist should be presented to him, and the choice fell upon Mr Phillips, who made a great impression. A. G. Gardiner, editor of *The Daily News*, wrote:

Mr J. S. R. Phillips, the editor of *The Yorkshire Post*, who has won all our hearts by his radiant good humour, was brought forward and began to talk about Lord Lonsdale, and to quote Heine to the Emperor. Mr Phillips will tell you that his German is wanting in two things – grammar and a vocabulary. But he can quote Heine with great unction, and he can make the simplest incident a subject of merry laughter.

When the first war news reached this country in August 1914, *The Yorkshire Post* announced in large heavy headlines, streaming now across two columns, 'Powers at War: European Conflict Opened'. The first leader spoke of the scientific advance which had contributed to the preparations for war and regretted the breakdown of all efforts towards international understanding; but added the opinion that 'there are times and conditions in which peace is impossible'. On Monday, 3 August, came news of the German invasion of France and Luxembourg and the Russian attack on Germany's right flank.

The same evening Sir Edward Grey made his famous speech in the House of Commons. It was fully reported in *The Yorkshire Post* on the morning of 4 August, and the first leader approved it as 'thoroughly statesmanlike'. The writer stressed once more the paper's consistent line of comment upon the value of friendship between England and Germany, but emphasized the nature of our obligations to France.

It was a week of swift action, and the newspaper's pages reflect the drama of the time. The German invasion of Belgium on 4 August was followed by the formal declaration of war between Great Britain and Germany. 'At war!', said the leader writer on the following morning. 'These fateful words were flashed last night to all our forces in all parts of the Empire and to our fleets – already cleared for action.' The forthcoming struggle was seen as pre-eminently a naval conflict.

As during the South African War, arrangements were made for a service of telegrams from the foreign correspondents of the various agencies and of *The Daily Telegraph*. The last named included the political letters of Dr E. J. Dillon, the foreign correspondent who as 'E. B. Lanin' had won fame for his striking articles on Russia in the *Fortnightly Review*. The *Daily Telegraph* dispatches were exclusive to *The Yorkshire Post* in the wide area over which the journal now circulated.

The First World War faced all newspapers with problems of newsprint, depletion of staff, and precautions against Zeppelin raids. *The Yorkshire Post* maintained a steady service to the public during these trying years. On certain days in the week the size of the morning paper was reduced to eight pages, and eventually it was found necessary to omit the lengthy 'Summary of the News' at the head of the leader column. On 1 April 1918 the price of the paper rose to twopence. A full general news service was provided and the chief features continued, with some notable advances in book reviewing. The literary page – The Library Table – began to show a lighter appearance, with shorter reviews and brief lists of other current publications. Walter Smith, the editor of The *Yorkshire Weekly Post,* helped with the book reviewing of the morning journal during the war years. Space was still given to music and art, and to dramatic criticism, and reports of agricultural and sporting events continued as usual. For the first time women were employed, and Lord Faber, the chairman, spoke warmly of their services during the emergency. When the news of the Armistice brought universal rejoicing, a leading article said:

We are not going to pass without praise the readiness with which women responded to the call for labour, to take the place of men who had gone to defend them . . . Mr Lloyd George, in addressing the crowd in Downing Street yesterday, said the war had been won by the 'sons and daughters of the people'. This is true, if in the phrase 'the people' the Prime Minister intended the whole of the people of this country, rich and poor, dukes and labourers; for certain it is that without the sons of those who sometimes have been the subject of undeserved depreciation, this war would never have been won.

John Phillips found much to disquiet his happy temperament in the mood of the new generation. The portrait inscribed 'The time is out of joint', taken as he stood, watch in hand, by the sundial in his garden, has its deep and abiding significance apart from the immediate reference to the Summer Time Act. In November 1919 he died suddenly as the result of a seizure, and the whole staff mourned the loss of an editor 'who was not only respected: he was loved'. A man of rare tolerance and kindliness, of scholarly serenity and spirited gaiety, J. S. R. Phillips left some delightful memories with his friends. One who worked with him wrote:

The Yorkshire Post may well be proud of an editor who has conducted the paper as he has conducted it during these years. He neither screamed nor wrung his hands; he never demanded anyone's head; he never made the work of statesman or soldier or sailor more difficult by embittered criticism. Sound, sober, helpful comment marked his words. He ground no party axe, nor did he yield to ignorant clamour.

The following January the Company's able and well-liked chairman, Lord Faber, resigned because of ill-health. He died on 17 September 1920. He had been one of Mr Phillips's greatest friends, and a perfect colleague in the direction of the newspaper. The relationship of directorate, staff, and management was that of a particularly happy family. On one occasion Mr Ben Turner (afterwards Sir Ben Turner), the well-known Socialist and trade union leader, visited the offices of *The Yorkshire Post*, and was impressed by the spirit that animated the staff. In the composing room he saw enthusiasm, speed, and energy such as (he said) he had not expected to discover in an establishment where the staff still worked on 'piece' rates. This respected trade union leader expressed the opinion that the method was good when it existed, as in the present instance, within the framework of friendly co-operation between management and staff. The system is retained in the composing room today, with equally valuable results.

Lord Faber was succeeded as chairman by his cousin the Hon. Rupert Evelyn Beckett, third and youngest son of the Company's first chairman, William Beckett. Rupert Beckett had served as a director since 1906. When in 1930 he received, as he expressed it, the 'supreme manifestation of civic regard' in the presentation to him of the Freedom of Leeds, he spoke in terms of special warmth of the long association of himself and his family with *The Yorkshire Post* and its allied papers.

The dissemination of knowledge and the cultivation of a sane outlook on affairs through the means of a clean and cultured Press has been one of the activities of which I am almost prouder than any other.

During his half century of service to the newspaper Rupert Beckett was known always for the eager interest which he took in even the smallest detail of office organization. To him the establishment was truly a family concern. Those who work on *The Yorkshire Post* hold him in honour and affection.

Educated at Eton and Trinity College, Cambridge, Rupert Beckett has always displayed qualities of intellect and temperament eminently suited for his great professional career. His eldest brother, Ernest William Beckett, succeeded his uncle by special remainder in the Grimthorpe barony; and his second brother, Gervase, had a distinguished political record, representing Whitby, then Scarborough and Whitby, and finally North Leeds in the House of Commons from 1906 to 1929. The duty of carrying on the business organization of Beckett's Bank fell, therefore, to Rupert Beckett. He gained experience of affairs of management at the headquarters of the Bank in Leeds and then, according to custom, as a junior member of the firm, took charge of the important Doncaster branch. After a period of military service as an officer of the Yorkshire Hussars, he came back to Leeds to take increased control of the Bank's headquarters with Lord Faber. When Beckett's Bank was amalgamated with the Westminster in 1921, Rupert Beckett and his elder brother, Gervase, became directors, and in 1931 Rupert Beckett was made chairman in succession to the late Mr Hugh Tennant. His business activity in Leeds led to close connexions with the Leeds Chamber of Commerce; and in 1909 he was made president of the Chamber, therein following the example of his brother Ernest and of his great-uncle, William Beckett. Such was the value placed upon his ability in this work that members persuaded him to fill the chair during three consecutive years.

CHAPTER VIII

After the First World War

[1919–1936]

The new editor was Arthur Mann, who left a key position in London, the editorship of the *Evening Standard*, to take up the appointment. He was chosen as a result of an interview with Rupert Beckett and his brother and fellow-director, Sir Gervase Beckett, Bt. Rupert Beckett had watched his notable editing of the *Evening Standard*, and in particular his introduction of its Londoner's Diary, which owed much to his contacts with leading men in political life. Mann was appointed editor of *The Yorkshire Post* in December 1919, and had charge of the paper for twenty years.

Arthur Mann is a native of the lovely old town of Warwick. He was the eldest of thirteen children of the late J. W. Mann, an alderman, Hon. Freeman and twice mayor of the town. His father was leader of the local Conservative Party and was a member of the town council for over forty years, so it was not unnatural that the eldest son took an early and abiding interest in municipal and national affairs. Arthur Mann was educated at Warwick School where he gained a reputation early as a cricketer, captaining the school team and scoring a century against King Edward's School, Birmingham. His journalistic career began with *The Western Mail* where he was articled for three years to Mr Lascelles Carr uncle of the late Sir Emsley Carr. Until he was made sub-editor of the firm's evening paper he played cricket for Glamorgan. Later appointments were to the staff of *The Birmingham Daily Mail*, and then to *The Birmingham Dispatch* as editor. From Birmingham he went to Fleet Street as London editor of *The Daily Dispatch*, Manchester. Soon afterwards he became editor of the *London Evening Standard*.

During the long period of his editorship of *The Yorkshire Post* he displayed outstanding qualities of courage, integrity, and independence: and these were matched by careful organization and preparation and the power to assume full responsibility for decisions on policy which were not always popular with the generality. Throughout his editorial career he showed acute political judgement, and on two notable occasions during his editorship the paper's influence was powerfully exercised. The first came in 1936 when, says Mr Ivor Thomas (writing on 'The Newspaper' in the *Oxford Pamphlets on Home Affairs*) '*The Yorkshire Post* set in motion the events leading up to the abdication of King Edward VIII'; the second was the paper's sustained opposition to the appeasement policy of Neville Chamberlain.

These episodes, which are fully described later, provide clear evidence of the paper's wide influence and of the editor's strength of character. *The Yorkshire Post,* already long-established as the leading journal ''twixt Trent and Tweed', was now not only an organ of national fame, but also one that was widely quoted on the Continent and in the United States. Mr Ivor Thomas's further comment is noteworthy:

There are two provincial newspapers, *The Manchester Guardian* published in Manchester, and *The Yorkshire Post* published in Leeds – which have relatively small circulations, but exert by sheer ability a national influence and must be regarded as national newspapers ... *The Manchester Guardian* and *The Yorkshire Post* are serious political newspapers with a national influence. Both are independent of national organizations, but the *Guardian* is the last stronghold of the Cobden School of Liberalism, and the *Post* expresses ''Twixt Trent and Tweed' a progressive Conservatism.

Describing *The Yorkshire Post*'s recent development in 'Provincial Newspapers in Transition' in *Alphabet and Image*, Mr S. L. Righyni, formerly of the staff of the *New York Herald Tribune* and later of that of *The Times*, notes also this 'free and honest expression of its views on policy which might be vital to this country'. Mr Righyni pays tribute both to Arthur Mann's wise and sound editorial guidance, and to the firm support given to him by the Company's chairman, the Hon. Rupert E. Beckett, and adds: 'It was that spirit, combined with outstanding technical accomplishment, which made *The Yorkshire Post* what it was'.

When, three years after his retirement, Arthur Mann became a Companion of Honour in the New Year Honours List, the Press made many appreciative comments on his twenty years' editorship, and *The Times* described him as an 'editor of independence and distinction'. There can be no doubt that future generations will see in him one of the pre-eminent figures in British journalism.

One who knows him and who became his successor has given this description of his personality:

At a first meeting Arthur Mann gives an impression of detachment. You like his tall, dignified figure, the meditative serenity, the courteous voice in discussion. They hint at a background of diplomacy rather than the excitement of newspaper work. You soon realize that here is rare and most valuable editorial strength – the strength of integrity ...

He dislikes the slipshod or hasty. He wants everything to be well thought out . . . The heavy organizing side of an editor's work prevented him from writing much direct for print. Nevertheless, the briefs he gave to his leader writers have been thorough and sometimes as long as the intended articles. When he has written a leading article himself every sentence has carried weight, every phrase has been telling. It was as though he kept himself poised and tense to strike the decisive blow in any political fight.

Although he was a determined antagonist of the new 'popular' journalism of the 'twenties and the 'thirties, Arthur Mann recognized the need for brightening the face of the morning paper, which still wore its late-nineteenth-century aspect. In February 1920 he gave titles to the leading articles and rearranged the London correspondence under the heading 'London Notes', subdividing the matter with side-headlines. 'The Library Table', Pebody's popular innovation, was still retained as the literary page's descriptive headline. Yet such is the conservatism of the human species that not all readers approved the editor's efforts on their behalf; on the introduction of titles to the leaders, a few irate correspondents wondered why their powers of comprehension were judged to have sunk so low as to need this extraneous guidance. In June 1928, when Mann produced his first picture page in the style of *The Times*, it was generally feared that the paper was about to lose its dignity, and there were many letters of protest; but within a few years the picture page became extremely popular. Its series of half-page photographs of Yorkshire scenes was particularly admired.

The journal had grown now to the size of fourteen to sixteen pages on weekdays and an eighteen-page issue on Saturdays. Advertisements had increased, often occupying as much as nine pages, while three pages were given to the markets and commercial news and a full page or more to sport.

On 3 December 1928 began the well-liked feature, 'This World of Ours', the title for which was chosen from the entries to a competition organized among the staff. This engaging column of notes was introduced by the original 'Northerner', F. A. Rice, with a modest manifesto declaring that the aim was 'to deal with topics of the day in a light and friendly manner'. Rice, not long down from Cambridge, where he had edited *The Granta*, brought a playful touch to his writing. Once again some staid readers protested; but 'This World' quickly won warm approval.

Rice was succeeded as 'Northerner' by H. W. Metcalfe, who lent his own gay and serene note to the column and gave it such an individual character that when he was called for service with the Royal Navy, shortly before the outbreak of the Second World War, it was decided to suspend publication of the feature. It was revived some months later when *The Yorkshire Post* was fused with *The Leeds Mercury*. The hope was that Metcalfe would resume editorship of 'This

World' after the war; but this spirited and delightful man was killed while serving with the Fleet Air Arm in 1943. He had been mentioned in dispatches for rescuing three of his comrades when the aircraft carrier *Eagle* was sunk. Since many readers identified 'Northerner' with Metcalfe, the pen-name was changed to 'Northerner II'. That signature still appears, but in fact, owing chiefly to exigencies of war, more than a dozen men have edited 'This World of Ours'. It has proved itself widely read and generally appreciated. Many after-dinner speakers have looked to it for stories.

In the domestic politics of the period *The Yorkshire Post* offered sound guidance. Arthur Mann's Conservatism was that of deep personal conviction and, like John Ralph, he tempered Party zeal by his profound belief that a political creed must adapt itself to changing conditions and that, in so adapting itself, its main consideration must be the national interest and not immediate Party advantage. One of his first important decisions, in the realm of economics, appeared to many as an augury of the abandonment of the traditional independence of *The Yorkshire Post*. The nation was involved in the great trade depression of the immediate post-war years and it was no longer possible, as during the first decade of the century, to advocate 'the system of allowing trade to take its natural course'. The United Kingdom was faced with a declining export trade and the powerful competition of cheaply-produced goods on foreign markets. After other leading Conservative journals had abandoned all advocacy of the old *laisser faire* economy in overseas trade, *The Yorkshire Post* still defended the principle of free and open competition, but conceded always the need for tariffs in certain instances. Arthur Mann now recognized that the country must adopt full protective measures if it were to regain its lead in world markets, and his realism produced a change of attitude which was not quite the *volte-face* that some critics considered.

Social problems were given close attention at this period. Slum clearance was now the primary concern of municipal authorities in the industrial north of England and the paper was in the vanguard of the fight to improve living conditions in the large towns. In 1920 its series of authoritative articles analysed such conditions in Leeds under the title 'The Physique of the Leeds People,' and 'Life in the Slums' was surveyed in every detail. In 1922 came a development that has proved a boon to the staffs of the company's newspapers. A sports club was founded with excellent playing fields and other amenities off Glen Road, Leeds.

On 19 October 1922 a meeting took place at the Carlton Club which was of great importance in the history of the Conservative Party. On the morning of the meeting *The Yorkshire Post* argued that the only hope for the Party lay in restoring

DISTINGUISHED DIRECTORS
PAST AND PRESENT

Sir Stanley Jackson (1870–1947), who was President of the Yorkshire County Cricket Club from 1939 to 1947, chairman of the Unionist Party 1923–6, and Governor of Bengal from 1927 to 1932.

Francis Alvey Rhodes Darwin (1851–1937), who was Clerk of the Peace for the West Riding from 1884 until his retirement in 1929, and Clerk to the West Riding County Council from 1888 to 1929.

Major R. S. Pearson (1872–1953), a prominent landowner and farmer in the North Riding.

Sir John Eaglesome (1868–1950), who played a notable part in the development of Nigeria.

The Hon. Sir Gervase Beckett (1866–1937), a banker and for many years a Member of Parliament.

Capt. A. K. Charlesworth (1892–1945), a colliery chairman. Capt. Charlesworth was killed in a flying accident while serving with the War Office in 1945.

T. L. Taylor, chairman of the Yorkshire Conservative Newspaper Company since 1950.

Sir Maxwell Ramsden, C.B., O.B.E.

Cecil Sagar-Musgrave.

Colin G. Forbes Adam, C.S.I., the present vice-chairman of the Company.

The Hon. Richard Wood, M.P. for Bridlington.

W. L. Andrews, the editor of The Yorkshire Post.

Ernest Osborn, the general manager of the Company.

Kenneth Parkinson.

its full independence. 'To Conservatives', said the writer, 'the question is not what will enable the Conservative Party at any cost to hold office, but what is for the good of the country and for the welfare of the Conservative Party that has a definite mission to perform in national life. We believe it will render its best service, and can only do so, by recovering its complete independence and entering the elections as a single fighting factor.' On the following morning the paper reported that the Unionist Members of Parliament at their Carlton Club meeting had, by a substantial majority, decided to leave the Coalition which had been in power so long and that Mr Lloyd George had resigned. There is no doubt that the result would not have been achieved but for Mr Bonar Law's attendance at the meeting which indicated his readiness to lead an independent Conservative Party. Bonar Law was not in good health at the time and he was very loath to assume heavy responsibility and also not unnaturally hesitated to put himself in opposition to the titular leader of the Party, Austen Chamberlain, who with F. E. Smith and other distinguished Conservatives supported the continuance of the Lloyd George Coalition. The editor of *The Yorkshire Post* in the days preceding the Carlton Club meeting paid several visits to Bonar Law at his London house to urge him to lead the anti-Coalition Conservatives, for Mann was convinced from his contact with rank and file Conservatives that most of them wished to see the Party regain its liberty of action and that this would be in the national interest. On the evening before the Carlton Club meeting he was one in a succession of callers which included Stanley Baldwin and other junior members of the Lloyd George Government who were imploring the reluctant statesman to attend the meeting on the morrow, but it was not until near midnight that Bonar Law at last came to a decision to attend.

In 1923 *The Leeds Mercury*, formidable rival of 1866, was at last brought into the family of the Yorkshire Conservative Newspaper Company, and this acquisition was to prove not only popular with the general public, but also of high significance in the history of *The Yorkshire Post*. During the century-long regime of the Baines family the *Mercury* had gained a prominent and honoured place in Yorkshire, and in Leeds particularly, where its name was identified with the city's life and progress. The famous editor T. W. Reid (later Sir Wemyss Reid) was one of the most ardent upholders of journalistic tradition. On one occasion W. T. Stead visited Reid, attempting to persuade him of the value of new methods. 'I see you think I am crazy', was Stead's comment – and from Reid came the guarded reply, 'Well, not crazy perhaps, but distinctly eccentric'.

Not until 1901, when the journal was bought by Lord Rothermere, was the austere make-up of *The Leeds Mercury* altered; but the change was sudden and dramatic. James Lumsden, the new editor, made it one of the most up-to-date papers of the day, using an elaborate technique of news display with many photographs as a daily feature. The price was lowered to a halfpenny, but it had been raised again to a penny before it was bought by the Yorkshire Conservative Newspaper Company. At the time of the purchase Lumsden relinquished the editorship and was succeeded by W. L. Andrews, one of Lord Northcliffe's young men, who had gone to London after much journalistic experience in his native Yorkshire and in Scotland and Paris.

Under the new editor's direction *The Leeds Mercury*, while remaining excellent for sport (with profitable racing tips by The Duke, Mr A. G. Thompson) and local news returned to some of its earlier traditions. It discussed political and economic questions with a lucidity and persuasiveness rare in journals of its kind. Many of its readers were Socialists, but they recognized the paper's respect for facts and liked it for its fairness and fighting qualities, especially when Hitler and Mussolini became enemies to the peace of the world. The paper developed into a great help to the Conservative cause.

Three years later the *Doncaster Chronicle* was acquired, in furtherance of a plan for printing localized editions in South Yorkshire of the *Evening Post*. The *Chronicle* had been founded in 1836 in a small room at the back of a bookshop opposite Doncaster's Mansion House. At that time Doncaster had no link by rail with important centres, and stage coaches still drove through its cobbled streets to the old hostelries which now remain as historic landmarks in the town. Set and folded by hand, and printed on an old Wharfedale flat-bed press at the rate of 400 copies an hour, this first *Chronicle* was an eight-page paper. Its proprietor-editor was Robert Hartley. Seventy years later the Doncaster Chronicle Printing and Publishing Company was formed by the Hon. Rupert Beckett and a group of men who shared his views. The headquarters were moved to the present site in Scot Lane. After its acquisition by the Yorkshire Conservative Newspaper Co. the *Chronicle* building was enlarged, up-to-date plant was installed, the staff was doubled, and the *Evening Post* was enabled to offer a later service of general news and an ampler supply of local news to its South Yorkshire readers. Mr Ernest Phillips, a man of vivid personality and overflowing energy, who had edited the *Chronicle* since 1908, remained as editor and also took charge of the Doncaster printed editions of the *Evening Post*. He held this joint responsibility until his retirement at the age of 76 in 1946. The duties that were his are fulfilled today by Mr J. R. Dibb.

Competition among the mass circulation papers was becoming fiercer and some of the methods called for criticism. Rupert Beckett spoke out strongly against them. Commenting on the catch-penny technique used when the circulation race was at its height, he observed drily: 'You bought a newspaper and you got an insurance policy, a stylo pen, a camera. It was all rather comic, there was no other word for it. These were days also when a big section of the newspapers gave snippets, and roared like the convicts at Dartmoor about nothing at all.' But *The Yorkshire Post* held steadily to its course; many years before, in 1913, Lord Northcliffe had remarked: 'I do not believe that *The Yorkshire Post* was ever stronger than it is today', and its solid foundations of independent ownership and commercial stability have proved enduring. On the news side *The Yorkshire Post* was well served at this time by William John Finnerty, who had been on the staff since 1883 and who succeeded William Leighton in the responsible position of news editor.

In December 1922 the general manager, Joseph Thornton, retired; he was succeeded by Arthur Grime, who moved over from the editorship of the *Evening Post*. Known in Leeds as 'a master maker of newspapers and a humanitarian', Mr Grime was remarkable for his service with equal success on both the editorial and the commercial sides. As editor of *The Yorkshire Evening Post* he is remembered publicly for his founding of the Boots for the Bairns fund. In 1928 he left Leeds to join his brother as joint governing director of the Blackpool Gazette and Herald Co. Ltd, and the management passed under the joint control of Mr E. H. Tillett and Mr Ernest Osborn. Mr Tillett had been general manager of *The Leeds Mercury*; he won the honour of election as president of the Newspaper Society during 1930. He was a firm upholder of the methods of sound newspaper production and had strong views on good advertising as opposed to any lowering of standards. Mr Ernest Osborn, a native of Leeds, has served the newspaper since 1901 and, as has already been mentioned, was private secretary for fifteen years to Joseph Thornton. His genial nature has won him wide popularity, and, for his part, he says today that of his fifty and more years with the Company he has enjoyed every moment, has found new interest every day, and has never ceased to marvel at the great spectacle of newspaper production on the technical side. Mr Osborn continued to serve as joint general manager throughout the war-time crisis, until Mr Tillett's retirement in September 1946. After that time he was to play an increasingly important part in the Company's history. Mr J. H. Bradley became assistant general manager in the changes of 1946.

To go back to 1926, the Company faced in May of that year one of the gravest crises in newspaper history: the General Strike. It arose out of the failure of the miners and the coal owners to reach an agreement within the four corners of the Coal Commission's report, published on 6 March 1926. The Government had announced its willingness to give effect to the Commission's recommendations if both parties would accept them. The representatives of the Trades Union

Congress, acting as mediators, recommended the miners to consider a wage reduction; but when they refused the T.U.C. called a general strike. As *The Yorkshire Post* put it, 'The T.U.C. were prepared to negotiate with the Government and the owners, but they were not prepared to place enough pressure on the miners to make their negotiations firm. They preferred to call a strike in support of a contention which they did not approve.'

News of this grave decision came on Monday, 3 May, close on midnight. Next morning a leading article said:

There has been no attack upon general wage standards. There has only been, first, an inability to carry on the coal industry under existing agreements, and next, the refusal of the miners to consider the proposed new agreement. It would be unjust to lay the whole blame for the deadlock upon the men. The dilatoriness of the owners has been a blameworthy factor in creating the eventual crisis. But there can be no question that the men's refusal to negotiate was the final cause of the break-up of the discussions. Because of that refusal the workers in other trades were called upon to break their legal agreements, to down tools, and to suffer and inflict suffering, without being allowed to express, or even to hold, an opinion of their own upon the merits of the dispute. If the workers at large realize just what is asked of them, and the affront which is placed upon them by this cavalier treatment, the way will be cleared for some compromise between the owners and the miners. While the General Strike is in operation, or threatened, that way will not, and cannot, be clear. Even now the fortunes of the country are at test. Democratic government is confronted by class dictatorship.

The T.U.C. now sought to silence the voice of the Press. But newspapers were produced, and high on the list of journals which maintained publication were *The Yorkshire Post* and its allied papers.

The approaching industrial crisis had been foreseen, and for some months the management had made careful preparations. Two empty warehouses were rented and filled with paper, and every available inch of space was packed with stocks of ink, packing paper, string, oil, stereo metal, and flong. Plans were made for delivery of the newspapers in Leeds and to more distant places by motor transport; these were augmented later when many volunteer helpers in Leeds and Yorkshire came in with their own cars. Methods of using to the best advantage the services of volunteers on the staff and of outside voluntary helpers had been decided upon. All who took part in this spirited campaign to maintain the services of the Press in the north of England were agreed that it was an exhilarating adventure.

The first paper to be published was *The Yorkshire Evening Post* of 4 May. *The Leeds Mercury* staff with their equipment were installed in the same offices as their *Yorkshire Post* colleagues, and a few minutes after midnight the two papers were being printed simultaneously at the rate of over 60,000 copies of each paper an hour. *The Yorkshire Post* comprised four pages, eight columns, and *The Leeds Mercury* two pages, six columns. It is a proud recollection of *The Leeds Mercury* veterans that their paper, a penny one, enjoyed for a day or two the largest sale in the country. At the end of the first week, *The Yorkshire Weekly Post* and *The Doncaster Chronicle* also maintained their publication.

In a letter to the editor the Prime Minister wrote:

I have been very pleased to see that you have been successful in maintaining the issue of your paper without any stoppage during the present crisis. It is an achievement of which you may well be proud, and I am sending you this line just to say how much I appreciate your help and support, which are in every way worthy of the splendid traditions of *The Yorkshire Post*.

Yours sincerely
(Signed) STANLEY BALDWIN

By 1933 the paper had established its policy, in face of all competition, as based upon 'the criterion of broad public interest', and the paper catered for the business and social life of the North, as well as for its intellectual and cultural life. Regular weekly features included Educational News, Theatres (preliminary announcements and reviews), the Cinema World, Nature Lover's Diary, Motorists and the Road, Bridge, Gardening, Music and Art, Sporting Notes, Agricultural Notes, the weekly Book Page, and the Week in Parliament. Parliamentary proceedings continued to be reported daily during sessions (except on Mondays), there were a daily picture page, the usual daily Foreign News, London Notes, financial and commercial articles, and special articles from experts. The journal offered much to appeal to a wide diversity of tastes in the North. The price continued to be twopence. In the words of Rupert Beckett the paper's constant aim was to 'offer an avenue for thought and ideas that make for a true appreciation of the important things of life'.

On 2 July 1934, at the Leeds University Degree Day ceremony held in the Town Hall, the editor of *The Yorkshire Post* was among the people eminent in various spheres of public life whose services the University desired to recognize; and Arthur Mann was the recipient of the honorary degree of LL.D., conferred by the Duke of Devonshire, then Chancellor of the University. Professor Hamilton Thompson, in introducing the editor, made reference to the valuable pioneer work of *The Leeds Intelligencer*, whose birthday by a happy chance fell on this degree day. That journal, he said, for more than a century built up the reputation which, under its later title, *The Yorkshire Post*, it had maintained and enhanced. He continued:

. . . today Leeds is justly proud of a daily paper which is everywhere recognized as upholding the best traditions of English journalism. Its influence within an area not immodestly claimed as extending from the Trent to the Tweed has been a powerful agent in the education of public opinion and enlightened taste. Its presentation of contemporary events, free from condescension to the allurements of sensationalism, is vivid and consistently accurate; its well-informed comments on topics of current interest are distinguished by sanity and moderation; while the competence of its literary and artistic equipment goes far to belie the popular superstition that the voice of the nightingale is never heard north of Trent.

After a brief reference to Arthur Mann's journalistic career and his mature conception of the dignity and responsibility of his vocation, Professor Hamilton Thompson spoke of the editor's employment of his chosen medium for the advancement of all causes which promote social and intellectual welfare, and ended with the simple and sincere tribute:

We in this University have good reason to thank him and his newspaper for the support which they have unfailingly given to our efforts and our claims, and no member of our community better deserves the honours which it is within our power to bestow upon merit.

Deeply moved by these references to *The Yorkshire Post*'s long and distinguished record, the editor wrote afterwards in *The Postscript*, the newspaper's house organ:

We have inherited a great tradition . . . To the quality of journalism that called forth praise on Degree Day all my colleagues contribute in their several capacities. Therefore, I took on the robes of Doctor of Laws proudly as representing my staff and as a public recognition that our kind of journalism is regarded by local leaders of thought and learning as a healthy and helpful influence in the social life of the north of England.

CHAPTER IX

The Abdication and increasing dangers

[1936–1939]

In 1936 King George V died, mourned deeply by all his subjects throughout the Commonwealth and Empire. Edward VIII was now King-Emperor, and the Coronation date was fixed for May 1937. In April 1936, a *Yorkshire Post* leader spoke of the meaning of the 'whole historic ritual in Westminster Abbey', a meaning outshining 'all the brave colour of flags and uniforms', and creating between the King and all his peoples 'a mutual bond giving rich meaning to the kingly office and rich promise to their common future'.

In December of that year, the abdication crisis broke upon the country and the full meaning of this mutual bond was made plain. For some time it had been known among newspapermen and in other circles that the King was often to be seen in the company of Mrs Simpson, an American woman who had obtained a decree *nisi* in an action for divorce against her husband on 27 October 1936. Although much gossip had been published on the subject in American newspapers, loyalty to the Crown and dislike of tittle-tattle about Royalty prevented any reference to it in the British Press. On 1 December occurred an event which faced editors with a grave decision. The Bishop of Bradford, referring in a public speech to the solemn meaning of the Coronation ceremony, used words of unmistakable significance.

In reporting such words, coming from a member of the Episcopacy of the Church of England, it was *The Yorkshire Post*'s duty to explain their import to its readers. This was done in a leading article on 'The King and His People', the responsible tone and the sober moderation of which will long be remembered and will, no doubt, go down in history:

The Bishop of Bradford said yesterday that the benefit to be derived by the people from the King's Coronation would depend in the first instance on 'the faith, prayer, and self-dedication of the King himself'. Referring to the moral and spiritual side of that self-dedication, the Bishop said the King would abundantly need Divine Grace if he were to do his duty faithfully, and he added: 'We hope that he is aware of his need. Some of us wish that he gave more positive signs of such awareness.'

Dr Blunt must have had good reason for so pointed a remark. Most people, by this time, are aware that a great deal of rumour regarding the King has been published of late in the more sensational American newspapers. It is proper to treat with contempt mere gossip such as is frequently associated with the names of European royal persons. The Bishop of Bradford would certainly not have condescended to recognize it. But certain statements which have appeared in reputable United States journals, and even, we believe, in some Dominion newspapers, cannot be treated with quite so much indifference. They are too circumstantial and have plainly a foundation in fact. For this reason, an increasing number of responsible people is led to fear lest the King may not yet have perceived how complete in our day must be that self-dedication of which Dr Blunt spoke if the Coronation is to bring a blessing to all the peoples of the Empire and is not, on the contrary, to prove a stumbling block.

On the same morning *The Leeds Mercury* also commented on the Bishop's speech and spoke of the responsibilities of a monarch who, by virtue of his exalted office, must give a moral example to the whole Empire. 'Britons everywhere', added the *Mercury*, 'love and honour their King. Their loyalty is spontaneous and vivid. For King Edward, as for his father, it is also intensely personal. It is based on recognition of his warmhearted sincerity, his honesty, and forthrightness. But our admiration and allegiance are not blind hero-worship. We do not accept the Stuart maxim: "The King can do no wrong".' These words were quoted all over the world.

The following day *The Times* quoted from *The Yorkshire Post* leading article and commented: 'It is a simple fact that the American campaign of publicity, so long and so wisely ignored in this country, has now reached a point at which it goes far beyond that side of his Majesty's life which may justly be held to be private'.

The rest of the painful episode of the abdication of a King well-beloved by his people has no place in this history. It is sufficient to say that *The Yorkshire Post* performed with reticence and dignity a most onerous duty; and if thereby it won national respect, that certainly could not have been foreseen at the difficult time of writing.

The age-long reverence of the British Empire for its ancient monarchy was preserved and was given full expression a year later in the Coronation of King George VI and Queen Elizabeth. In honour of the new reign *The Yorkshire Post* issued a Coronation Supplement of sixty-four pages, with an excellent photographic display and special articles, notably an analysis of the meaning of the Coronation ritual by Dr Temple, Archbishop of York. The daily issue of Thursday, 13 May, contained seven full picture pages showing festivities in Leeds and Yorkshire, and Arthur Bryant wrote his impressions of the 'glittering picture of Westminster Abbey' in 'The King in His Hour of Dedication'. A leading article commented on the new miracle of wireless, whereby 'for the first time in the world's history yesterday it was literally true that a King and Emperor took his Coronation Oath and received acclamation and homage in the ears of all the peoples and the nations.' The 'London Notes and Comment' had a side-headline 'Television makes history', but noted that 'Broadcasting is for the millions; television – as yet – for the hundreds'. Only sixteen years later television's magic was to bring the millions within range of the Abbey Ceremony itself.

The episode for which Arthur Mann's editorship of *The Yorkshire Post* will be chiefly remembered is his long and determined stand on foreign policy. In making this stand he agreed with Mr Eden's attitude, but the rumour sometimes heard, that that statesman, having married a niece of the chairman of the company, had a decisive influence in laying down the policy for the paper was quite wrong. Arthur Mann did his own thinking. From 1935 onwards events in Europe moved rapidly towards a climax in crisis after crisis, as the German and Italian dictators kept the whole world in a state of nervous expectation by their predatory acts and deceptive phrases. The situation was delicate and obscure, and in countries where democratic sentiment was strong there was often sympathy for the social aspirations and the economic grievances loudly reiterated by the Fuehrer and his satellite. Memoirs of the time are growing, but are not yet complete. Sir Winston Churchill's record of 'the Second World War' is the classic of this generation, and the recently published memoir of Viscount Norwich (better remembered as Mr Duff Cooper) is an invaluable piece of firsthand evidence. Future studies will, no doubt, be written with more detachment, but less insight into an epoch which is surely unprecedented in the annals of history.

It is common knowledge that during these critical years *The Yorkshire Post* by its forceful expression of opinion became one of the most generally respected journals of the day, both at home and overseas. From the outset, the paper insisted that it was only by means of collective action, through the appropriate machinery of the League of Nations, that European peace could be secured. With regard to German claims it declared: 'We may recognize fully the sense of national worth and capacity which Hitlerism has inspired in Germans. We should not deny the contributions which a fit and confident nation can make to the progress of the World.' Germany's choice of government was not our concern, but her racial and religious intolerance offended public opinion in this country. Therefore, if there were to be peace between the two nations there must also be frankness; and Germany should show her willingness to take part in League methods of international co-operation.

On the subject of the League itself, *The Yorkshire Post* considered that it must combine strength with elasticity. There must be united resistance to aggression, but such resistance should be accompanied by evidence of the desire to find remedies for legitimate grievances. Collective deliberations and collective decisions were demanded. 'We cannot swerve from that policy', said the paper, 'without damaging our prestige and without plainly betraying those countries which so far have gone with us in pursuit of League policy.' Critics of the League, it added, 'do not appear to appreciate the immense importance for the future of demonstrating that there does exist a collective body, even if it is incomplete, which opposes the conscience of Christendom and of civilization to a war of aggression, but which is at the same time "elastic", that is, able and willing, so far as it can, to try and find remedies for legitimate complaints'.

The weakness of Britain was seen as the cause of the lack of confidence in League methods in Europe, and therefore the paper advocated a vigorous policy of rearmament, in order that this country might be equipped for her important mediatorial role. Then Germany could make her choice, and if she chose isolation it was foolish to complain of 'encirclement' by nations which had adopted the collective method. Geographically she might become encircled, but it would be by her own free will. When the Socialists denounced the policy of rearmament, *The Yorkshire Post* commented:

The opposition of idealists, such as Mr George Lansbury, to any policy involving the maintenance of arms under national control is intelligible even if it is Utopian. The other kind of opposition, as a mere matter of political opportunism, is unintelligible, and is not likely to commend itself to the common sense of the community.

It may be noted here that not only Socialists were sternly warned of their grave responsibilities during this period. In November 1936 the Premier, Mr Stanley Baldwin, confessed to the House of Commons with what he described as 'appalling frankness' that he had deferred to public opinion at the time when pacifist feeling was strong, recognizing that the country would not rally to a call for rearmament. *The Yorkshire Post* acknowledged that Mr Baldwin had a case for what he had done; he had feared that to speak out at that moment would mean the return of a Socialist Government which would neglect the country's defences. But the paper added:

Even when political defeat is probable, still it cannot be the duty of the country's elected leaders to keep silence on matters vital to the very existence of the nation and Empire. The consequences of their meek submission to ignorant popular sentiment may be infinitely more grave than would be temporary defeat of themselves and their programme.

This rebuke to a respected Conservative leader offers further evidence of the independence that characterized Arthur Mann's editorship and the strong sense of public duty which always guided his comments.

The urgent need for a rearmament drive had been revealed in March when Hitler had occupied the demilitarized zone of the Rhineland: an action which was not only a repudiation of the military clauses of the Treaty of Versailles, but also a flagrant violation of the Locarno Pact. Writing on the gravity of the situation, *The Yorkshire Post* said:

... We cannot insulate ourselves against the effects on the Continent, because the peace of Europe may be endangered by this action, and the peace of Europe is Britain's most immediate personal concern. Least of all can we be indifferent to Germany's action as it affects League principles ... If Germany thinks she can take her present action with impunity it is only because she is trading on the spirit of peace in other European countries ... We believe Herr Hitler has depended to a very large extent upon the known desire of the Government and the people of this country to seek peace and ensue it, and in all circumstances to prefer conciliation and negotiation to the pre-war methods of provocation. Certainly that is the spirit of the whole country. In that spirit, doubtless, we shall attempt, not indeed to excuse German action, but to see whether under this provocation there may be some means whereby we can assist to avoid the catastrophe which German action has brought dangerously near.

However, with the bland air of the burglar turned policeman, Hitler now proposed to bring Germany back into the League, professing satisfaction with his spoils. The now familiar technique was not familiar then, and many were deceived by his fair protestations of peaceful intentions. *The Yorkshire Post* continued, as before, to emphasize the urgent necessity of firm and concerted action based upon the sanctity of international law:

Germany has broken a voluntary treaty and violated her undertaking to resort to arbitral procedure in case of dispute regarding its interpretation. And yet she proposes to rejoin the League, whose fundamental principle is arbitral procedure. We must most earnestly hope that Germany, by wisely-considered statesmanship, which is more than mere protestation, will make it possible for her neighbours to take up with her more confidently the problem of putting European peace once more upon a stable foundation.

There followed a defence debate in Parliament, in the course of which Mr Churchill and Mr Lloyd George advocated special security measures; the latter going so far as to advance the plea for Government direction of war-time research and industry. This policy, unpopular at first with a large and indefinable cross-section of public opinion, found support in *The Yorkshire Post*, which commented: 'We pay a price for democracy. If it is not to be too high, then the people themselves must rally without reserve to the support of the Government in the taking of measures whose urgent necessity has been fully explained.'

A further meeting of the Locarno Powers showed that Germany intended to indulge in mere words, without evidence of any desire towards restitution. Vainly the paper argued that 'the country must show, beyond any shadow of doubt, that it stands firmly with the other members of the League in refusing to condone the Rhineland coup. If there were any failure on this account, the whole of the collective system would be shattered.'

Although the initiative in this long campaign to persuade the Western democracies to stand up to the dictators was taken by a strong-minded and clear-sighted editor, the part played by his chief leader writer, Charles Tower, in its pursuit should not be overlooked. Tower, a product of Marlborough and Oxford, and a brilliant classical scholar, had a profound knowledge of international affairs and of Germany in particular. He had served as *Daily Mail* correspondent in Berlin before the First World War, and he had seen something of the temper of the German authorities and people when that war came. He was observing a wild scene in Berlin in 1914 when a blow from a policeman's truncheon crippled him for life. Knowing so much of certain aspects of the German mentality at first hand, he was never deceived by Nazi propaganda as were so many in the middle 'thirties.

While Hitler's treacheries multiplied, Mussolini was pursuing a policy of active intervention in the Spanish Civil War and of open aggression in Abyssinia; and in 1937 the two dictators showed plainly the firmness of the Berlin-Rome Axis, as it was called, at their meeting in Berlin. Reporting the result of the interview, Mussolini declared: 'The Fuehrer and I can answer with a loud voice – Peace!' The British Government, under Mr Baldwin, at last announced a great rearmament programme and set to work on it at once. There was some protest from the Opposition, but by now public opinion was beginning to recognize the necessity, and the welcome extended to defence preparations was unmistakable. The great factor was time.

At the beginning of 1938 Hitler succeeded in overcoming Mussolini's previous objections to the destruction of Austrian independence, and in February took place his historic interview with Schuschnigg at Berchtesgaden. Immediately after Schuschnigg returned he gave an interview to L. R. Muray, who was at the time *The Yorkshire Post* representative in Vienna and in confidence told him that during his meeting with Hitler the Fuehrer banged the table and shouted, 'I shall always get my way because I am ready to run the risk of war and my opponents are not'. Muray at once passed on this information by letter to the editor and it confirmed Mann in his conviction that the policy of appeasement would only encourage aggression. On 11 March German troops marched into Austria, prevented the free plebiscite arranged to take place on union, and a month later produced a 99.7% majority for union with Germany. All was complete before anything could be done about it.

All this time in England events were leading up to the resignation of the Foreign Secretary, Anthony Eden, in disagreement with the foreign policy of the new Prime Minister, Neville Chamberlain. It was not generally known then, though revealed later by Sir Winston Churchill and Mr Sumner Welles, that among the major reasons for the Foreign Secretary's resignation was that during his absence on holiday in the South of France Mr Chamberlain had declined President Roosevelt's offer, made on 12 January 1938, to call a conference at Washington of representatives of the European States at which an attempt might be made to find a peaceful solution of outstanding disputes and difficulties. In the course of his resignation speech in the House of Commons, Mr Eden made a veiled allusion to a further cause of disagreement with the Prime Minister's policy, but could not be more explicit out of regard for the confidential nature of the President's proposal. It seems probable that at this stage Mr Chamberlain was trying an experiment. He was seeking to replace the crumbling system of collective security with a four-power pact, designed to bring Germany and Italy into the position of good Europeans. In London Von Ribbentrop, the German Ambassador, assiduously fanned these hopes, and in 1937 Lord Halifax went to see Hitler to try to find some means of inaugurating a general movement for the redress of grievances and the reduction of armaments. The effect of this visit was negative. Indeed, soon afterwards Mussolini took Italy out of the League. The day of Mr Eden's resignation was chosen by Hitler to attack the democracies in a lengthy peroration, and next day German Press headlines said, in effect, 'Hitler Speaks, Eden Goes'. There followed the invasion of Austria, already described, and in May the German mobilization against Czechoslovakia, deterred by a veiled warning from London and Paris. Then came the famous demands of Henlein on behalf of the Sudeten Germans, and the mission of Lord Runciman to Prague.

During this procession of events *The Yorkshire Post* had continued its constructive criticism on foreign policy, recognizing the complexity of the situation and the fact that Great Britain had been manoeuvred into a difficult situation by the duplicity of the two dictators. Her intervention in the Sudeten question, it was considered, was a tacit acceptance of moral responsibility and should, therefore, be followed up by a diplomatic and military understanding with France and Russia. Such action, it was felt, might enable Britain even yet to lead Europe by strong statesmanship to a just settlement of grievances and the abandonment of war as an instrument of policy. When the Prime Minister made his decision to go in person to Munich and meet Herr Hitler and found himself obliged to cede the latter's demands, it was noted that even this humiliating surrender to superior force had been necessitated by the unpreparedness of this country, and particularly London, against air attack. *The Yorkshire Post* did not say that Mr Chamberlain could have done otherwise in the course that he had chosen; but the paper had consistently questioned the wisdom of the actions which had led up to the situation. After Munich, the journal continued this line of comment and criticized the soundness of the policy which the Prime Minister was still pursuing. It is well known that this independence of opinion called forth admiration on the one hand and sharp criticism on the other. But the paper's object was neither praise nor blame. As an editorial put it:

In expressing these views our aim throughout has been to contribute to national unity and strength. To keep silence on causes of dissension and distrust cannot further this aim, and would be nothing less than a failure in patriotic duty.

Among the men who helped to formulate policy and give distinction to *The Yorkshire Post* under Arthur Mann's editorship were such leader writers as the late Charles Tower, already mentioned; Collin Brooks, who later became editor of *Truth* and has won a wide reputation as a broadcaster; Charles Davy, now assistant editor of the Sunday *Observer*; Iverach McDonald, now foreign editor of *The Times*; Hugh Ross Williamson, who left to edit *The Bookman* and to become a national name in broadcasting; and the late R. K. Bacon, who became adviser on public relations to the Prime Minister.

The post-Munich editorial comment of the paper now became one of the subjects most widely discussed, both in Yorkshire and in the north of England. At a meeting of the executive committee of the York Conservative Association in November 1938 a protest resolution was passed, deploring 'the anti-Government attitude adopted by *The Yorkshire Post*', and expressing the opinion that 'the present policy of *The Yorkshire Post* is doing a signal disservice to the country in general and to the Conservative Party in particular'. Some letters had also appeared in the paper's correspondence columns advancing similar views, and the journals' editorial comments were the subject of certain unfavourable remarks at various Conservative meetings throughout the county. Nevertheless, the editor stood firm. In December 1938 an article entitled '*The Yorkshire Post* and Foreign Policy' replied to critics described as 'Conservatives who are surprised to see a Conservative newspaper attacking the policy of a Conservative Prime Minister'. Recapitulating its outstanding comments of past months, *The Yorkshire Post* answered: 'Nothing could finally harm the prestige of the Conservative Party more than that it should, for the sake of a Party advantage, continue to give blind support to a policy which is so gravely endangering national interests as a whole'.

Letters, for and against the paper's attitude, continued to pour into the office, indicating the degree of public anxiety concerning the whole subject of peace and war. Many readers emphasized the need for collective action against the dictators, for the awakening of a Christian conscience in face of the brutal persecution of the Jews in Germany, for the 'leader of vision, who will call upon his countrymen to accept the risks incidental to the principle of arbitration'. Others favoured the course taken by Chamberlain: if he had not acted as he did, one reader said, 'today our country would have been ravaged by a terrible war, the consequences of which are unthinkable'.

On 3 January 1939 *The Yorkshire Post* published an editorial under the title 'A Newspaper's First Duty', which pointed out that neither official pressure nor Party loyalty should restrain a newspaper from 'telling the public the full truth about current events to the best of its power'.

In appreciation of the paper's views A. J. Cummings of *The News Chronicle* wrote three days later in his feature column 'Spotlight on Politics':

The Yorkshire Post (leading Conservative organ in the provinces, which has criticized the Chamberlain policy with great courage and consistency) published on Tuesday a magnificent editorial on the functions of the Press. It would not be a bad thing if the article could be framed and hung prominently on the wall above the desk of every newspaper editor and proprietor in the country.

In February 1939, the matter, very naturally, formed the chief topic of discussion at the Company's Annual General Meeting, and there were the inevitable conflicts of opinion. The journal's recent editorial policy was vigorously defended by the chairman of the Board of directors, the Hon. Rupert E. Beckett, who declared that criticisms of the Government's foreign policy were not in any sense due to lack of allegiance to the Conservative Party, but to conclusions definitely arrived at after a collation of information gathered by men of experience at home and abroad. Expressing the view that subsequent events had vindicated the paper's conclusions, he made a notable speech in support of editorial independence and due freedom of expresssion:

In so far as you ask me to say anything which will tie the hands of this newspaper and prevent it from giving free and honest expression of its views on policy which may be vital to this country, I shall not sit here and consent to that.

Such an attitude was of inestimable importance, and on the day following the publication of the report of the chairman's statement, a correspondent wrote appreciatively: 'While that spirit animates those who exercise a guiding influence on *The Yorkshire Post* – one of the finest, if not the best, morning papers in the country – we have nothing to feel uneasy about'.

The Yorkshire Post had fought a great battle for the liberty of the Press, and its national reputation as a powerful organ of expression may best be summed up in the words of a leading article which appeared in *The Manchester Guardian* on 28 November 1939:

Soundness in judgement, tenacity of purpose, loyalty to principle, the courage to be unpopular – which, with another sort of journalism, is a folly where it is not a crime – and even to offend the Party if the Party were not right; these qualities, which are the more precious for being rare, have marked *The Yorkshire Post* throughout the long controversy about British foreign policy which began with Mr Chamberlain's Premiership. They represent something deep in the characteristic North, tough, earnest, individual. The country owes a debt for them to the old *Yorkshire Post*.

Arthur Edward Grime, general manager of the Company from 1923 to 1928.

W. J. Finnerty, a news editor of The Yorkshire Post, *who joined the paper as a boy in 1883 and served with it for 55 years.*

Sir John Foster Fraser, Parliamentary sketch writer and special correspondent of The Yorkshire Post *in the early part of the present century.*

Dr Herbert Thompson, Art and Music Critic of The Yorkshire Post *from 1886 to 1936. From the portrait by Malcolm Osborne.*

A. W. Pullin ('Old Ebor'). On his retirement in 1931 he had been chief cricket and football writer of The Yorkshire Post *for nearly forty years.*

Edward Tillett, joint general manager of the Company from 1928 to 1946.

Charles Tower, leader writer before the Second World War, who wrote many of the anti-appeasement leading articles.

A. G. Thompson, 'The Duke' of The Leeds Mercury, who had a great following among racegoers. He contributed to The Yorkshire Post.

Alan Woodward, editor of The Yorkshire Evening Post *since 1949.*

Ernest Phillips, editor of The Doncaster Chronicle *from 1908 to 1946.*

J. R. Dibb, editor of The Doncaster Chronicle *and the South Yorkshire editions of* The Yorkshire Evening Post.

Joe Illingworth, Yorkshire Post *war correspondent in the Second World War and now London editor.*

CHAPTER X

Joining forces: a broader appeal

[1939–1945]

1754–1954: Two centuries are past, but the editorial voice has not changed its tone. Where Griffith Wright appealed for support as 'the reader's most obedient humble servant', the present editor continued to avow his constant aim to be in all things 'the servant of the public'. The story is one of incessant effort, of strife renewed and at last resolved. In 1754 *The Leeds Intelligencer* and *The Leeds Mercury* were at war. In 1755 the latter was dead. In 1767 a resurrected *Mercury* re-entered the fray and within a century had forced the emergence of *The Yorkshire Post*. At last came the combination of the dignified and respected *Yorkshire Post* and the lively, warm-hearted *Mercury*, with W. L. Andrews as the first Yorkshireman to occupy the editorial chair of *The Yorkshire Post*. So ended the rivalry of two newspapers which, having fought their several battles against the problems and hazards of nearly two hundred years, found strength in unity and together confronted the most difficult years in the history of British journalism.

The question of welding the two dailies into one paper had been receiving serious consideration for some years before 1939. Public taste had changed. The increasing tempo of life was leaving less and less leisure for reading the older style of newspaper and had strengthened the demand for summarized news and easy entertainment. At the same time improved methods of communication carried the national newspapers of whatever calibre further and more quickly afield. All these developments were steadily restricting the demand for which regional newspapers had so long catered. In 1860 the provincial public wanted local journals in order that they might have early news of events in London and abroad. In 1930 this need was met to some extent by papers published in London or Manchester and reaching the chief northern centres a few hours later.

But there was a demand in a region like that 'twixt Trent and Tweed for a morning paper giving much more space to local news than a national daily could afford. *The Yorkshire Post* and *The Leeds Mercury*, issued from the same office, were trying to meet this demand in different ways: *The Yorkshire Post* at twopence with a traditional emphasis on the full-dress treatment of politics, the *Mercury* at a penny with a light and picturesque touch and not much room for solidity. If the two papers could be combined without any serious loss of their sharply different sets of readers, a difficult problem would be solved. But there was a formidable risk in making so great a change, for there might be incompatible elements in the two circulations, and a decision was postponed until the exigencies of war brought the matter to a head. Many restrictions were already harassing the newspaper world in 1939, and rising prices, especially of newsprint, necessitated the strictest economies in output and working costs. Racing and all forms of sport in this country were abandoned, thereby adversely affecting newspapers. In these circumstances a committee was appointed by the Board of directors, which formed the unanimous decision that the best course to pursue in view of such problems was to amalgamate the two morning papers and to issue the combined paper at the price of one penny. The plan was duly put into execution, and on Monday, 27 November 1939, appeared the first issue of the combined paper under the dual title of *The Yorkshire Post and Leeds Mercury*.

As the Hon. Rupert Beckett told shareholders at the company's Annual meeting in March 1940, this decision was arrived at only after very careful deliberation; and one of the factors to be considered was displacement of staff. 'Obviously one paper requires considerably fewer people to produce than two', he said, 'Consequently, there was bound to be – and, indeed, had to be, if projected economies were to be effective – some displacement. The recommendation of the committee of directors was to the effect that compensation to staff displaced should be paid on the most generous scale that our Company could afford.' To supplement this payment Mr Beckett made a personal gift of £5,000. The many letters of thanks and appreciation testified to the justice and generosity with which the inevitable changes were effected.

At the same meeting Rupert Beckett explained that the editor of *The Yorkshire Post,* Arthur Mann, 'regarded the future of our newspapers, as designed by the Board, with considerable misgiving' and did not disguise the fact when war came, with its numerous additional complexities for the newspaper world. 'In these circumstances', said Mr Beckett, 'it was amicably agreed that he should relinquish the burden; consequently, he has retired from his post as editor, and we one and all wish him well'. Taking up his residence in London, Arthur Mann continued his active interest in national affairs and in the Conservative cause;

he was made a Companion of Honour in 1941. From that year until 1946 he served as a Governor of the B.B.C. and contributed many useful ideas in the development of broadcast programmes.

In introducing the editor of the combined journal, Rupert Beckett said: 'His successor is Mr W. L. Andrews, who for several years has edited *The Leeds Mercury* with great ability. He is well known in Leeds and the West and East Ridings, and I am sure his many friends will welcome the advent of W. L. A. to the editorial chair of our now combined morning papers.'

William Linton Andrews is a native of Hull, son of the late William Andrews, a publisher and author and editor of the Bygone Series of books. Educated at Hull Grammar School and at Christ's Hospital, London and West Horsham, W. L. Andrews trained as a reporter and at the age of 20 became a free lance correspondent in Paris. In the first week of the 1914 war he joined the Black Watch, and while serving for three years on the Western Front contributed largely to *The Daily Mail*. With a comrade, J. B. Nicholson, he wrote the first description of the Battle of Neuve Chapelle to appear in print. Lord Northcliffe, pleased with such enterprise, invited him to join the staff of *The Daily Mail* as soon as he could. Andrews was a sub-editor of this paper for five years, and in 1923 was invited by The Yorkshire Conservative Newspaper Company to take over the editorship of *The Leeds Mercury*.

He has often broadcast on news of the North and on newspaper problems, and occasionally took part in the B.B.C. Brains Trust. During the Second World War he was chairman of a provincial editors' committee and as such in close liaison with the Government. He is a past president of the Institute of Journalists and of the Guild of British Newspaper Editors, and vice-chairman of the Press Council, which he did much to bring about. He has been described as the father of the Press Training Scheme, which he advocated for many years. In 1950 he was appointed a director of the Yorkshire Conservative Newspaper Company.

It was a formidable task that had to be faced by the new editor of the combined newspaper. Not only was he taking over the mantle of a great predecessor with a world-wide reputation, but the dust of the bitter controversy on foreign policy of 1938–40 was not yet laid, and there were too many people who saw in the recent change an aftermath of that political dispute. In fact the reasons which had led to the change were purely economic, but such a background made the new pilot's task no easier, especially when he had also to face the unpredictable conditions of a world war which was now drawing the whole national life into its service. Steady courage, sound judgement, and outstanding ability were needed to meet and overcome all these difficulties.

Certain changes in make-up were necessary in the combined paper and of these the one to evoke the greatest reaction from readers was the decision to give news on the front page. As was explained to 'faithful old readers', this was not the unprecedented innovation that it seemed: front page news in *The Yorkshire Post* dates back to 1866, although in a form that would make little appeal to twentieth-century readers. The practical purpose behind the change was that of satisfying busy men and women who now had to read their morning paper in crowded trams, trains, or buses. At a glance the full war news could be seen on the front page, while the chief items of Yorkshire interest were on the back page. Such features as Parliamentary, agricultural, and commercial notes could then be studied in what leisure time was still available.

The problem set the editor and his staff at the start was how to meet the tastes of readers both of *The Yorkshire Post* and of *The Leeds Mercury* in a restricted war-time paper. It was happily solved by continuing to meet *The Yorkshire Post* readers' demand for political and commercial news while making a much broader appeal to readers generally.

In his article on 'Provincial Newspapers in Transition', to which reference has already been made, S. L. Righyni sees the combination of the two papers as an example of modernization without loss of dignity; and on the changed appearance of the front page he is wholly commendatory:

Its front page is a page that can be read without a break. The reader is rarely asked to continue a message inside the paper. If matter connected with an item on the front page has to be printed inside – the text of a speech of which extracts have been printed on the main page, for instance – he is always directed to it by a cross-reference. In this the paper is particularly considerate of its readers' comforts.

The writer observes also that 'the achievement of a sale – a restricted sale – of more than 160,000 copies a day is evidence that this presentation is proving popular in its area.' He could not know how much relief that achievement brought to the Board of directors, who had taken their decision to amalgamate upon an estimate of a probable daily circulation of 65,000 copies and who saw the sales rising steadily month after month. This success was one of the outstanding journalistic achievements of war-time.

The change did not satisfy everyone, and letters of criticism as well as messages of thanks were received. One writer applied such epithets as 'loathsome' and 'horrible' to the alteration, and said that he had not 'the heart to read the present enormity': to which the editor rightly replied that 'if he has not read the paper, as he says, his criticism cannot be of much value'. Another sent his support, and added 'more power to your elbow', while yet another considered the combined journal 'a promising young fellow who deserves a better deal'.

'Why not call him The Yorkshire Mercury?', he asked. As the editor pointed out, such a departure would not 'sufficiently indicate the two historic papers that now are one'.

Mr Righyni, noting also this divergence of opinion between those who said 'I miss the little *Mercury*' and others who said 'Give me the old *Yorkshire Post*', considered that 'both groups are justified in their view; but what both groups have to remember is that their combined newspaper has had to meet not only the difficulties of combination, but also those of newsprint shortage', and he concluded his detailed analysis by explaining that 'the Leeds example has been examined in some detail because it is proof of the opportunity that exists for responsible ownership and sympathetic editing'. His article was written in January 1948, after *The Yorkshire Post and Leeds Mercury* had weathered successfully the many difficulties which were to mark its first decade of development.

The first and most acute of these was the shortage of newsprint and its rising cost. After the outbreak of the Second World War, on 3 September 1939, the situation became baffling in its complexity. There was an immediate and heavy decrease in advertising revenue, together with a rise in production prices. Circulation figures were maintained and increased by the eager public demand for war news; but this demand had to be met at a time when outside factors were operating towards restricted sales and petrol rationing was multiplying delivery problems.

Reliable and forthright comment on the grave news of the day was the primary desire of the community. Yet fewer editions could be published, and all newspapers found themselves obliged to reduce their sizes by about forty per cent.

In July 1940 the morning journal took on a 'new look', which was in some respects reminiscent of the old look of its early forebears. A slightly narrower column was introduced so that one page could contain eight columns of news, thereby gaining a column a page. The Ionic type face introduced in June 1932 now proved its easy readability. At the same time the size of *The Yorkshire Post* was reduced to six pages in common with that of all other penny papers. The following year brought staff depletions: 385 of the staff of the whole concern were already serving with the Forces, and forty-seven were engaged on munitions or on Government work. Yet during this difficult year the sales of the morning paper increased, and its influence and prestige were maintained. 'Hitler's War has had many strange effects', said the editor: 'one of the strangest is that large sales, instead of being the desired goal, have become a serious embarrassment to newspapers'.

It became necessary, in time, to cut down circulation in order to enable a larger paper to appear on Saturdays, giving the estate and auction sales announcements which were an essential part of the life of the region. This decision was taken with deep reluctance. It meant causing bitter disappointment to many readers who could not understand why they should have to go without a paper they had bought and loved almost all their days.

As reductions in size and changes in make-up were necessitated they were carefully explained to readers. The first newsprint scarcity was a direct result of shipping problems, since most of the paper had to come from North America and had to take second place to food and munitions. But the journal had a well-formulated policy. In March 1941, it stated:

Experience gained during the last war shows that skilful sub-editing and management can help to produce an excellent paper even in small space. We hope to avoid the danger of producing a sheet like a bulletin from a tape machine. We shall keep in the features that have built up the staunch character of *The Yorkshire Post* and we shall continue to exercise to the full the right of democratic journalism.

To the great relief of many faithful readers it added 'and we shall print crossword puzzles when we can'. Despite the extraordinary difficulties such cultural features as book reviews and music and art notices were kept going, though the book notices shrank to a monthly column at one period. Such services did not go unnoticed. In a report by PEP (Political and Economic Planning) published in 1946, *The Yorkshire Post* was mentioned among the small group of papers whose art criticism continued to be authoritative and influential. Another enterprise of value was the publication of a series of articles on the application of scientific research to industry. These were reprinted in a pamphlet.

The newsprint situation worsened when the Nazi invasion of Norway cut Britain off from one of her main sources of supply of wood pulp.

In November 1942, two years to the day after *The Yorkshire Post* was fused with *The Leeds Mercury*, it was announced that circulation figures were close upon 100,000 copies daily, and surpassed that figure on Saturdays. In the same year the paper's national reputation was made evident when Lord Camrose quoted its views in the House of Lords during a debate on the freedom of the Press. He said: 'There are not so many provincial papers that have commented on the matter, but I am going to read to the House extracts from two of the most serious-minded in the country'. They were *The Yorkshire Post* and *The Birmingham Post*.

During the war years the leading articles of the morning paper were publicly commended on many occasions for their fearless candour and sober recognition of the gravity of the news. The editor, as he sought to do everything possible to end the schism which the appeasement issue had caused in the Conservative Party, was fortunate in one respect. He had a policy with which every reader could agree – that of making the paper of the utmost service in the drive for victory. Frank and searching criticism was often printed of different aspects of the war effort; but this criticism was always designed to help. Constructive suggestions were put forward, and were frequently adopted by Government departments alert to improve their administration. An example was the editor's proposal for men from the battle areas to visit the war factories to tell workers of the part their munitions were playing in the fight. This was done, with excellent results. Women who had made screws without the slightest knowledge of their ultimate purpose were thrilled to know they were used in the tanks that were in the hottest forefront of the battle. Up went output.

The outspoken comment of the paper, both before and during the war, angered enemy governments and in September 1945, an editorial remarked with interest upon the revelation that it figured in the Gestapo list of thirty-five British publications whose offices were to be seized, their records confiscated and their executives arrested immediately upon the completion of the projected Nazi invasion of this country. 'We may take it as a tribute', said the writer, 'that our policy was disliked in the circles around the Fuehrer'.

In these years *The Yorkshire Post* upheld in its columns the democratic ideals that were threatened by the emergence of military dictatorships. 'Hitler has repeatedly sneered at our democracies', said a leading article in 1940, 'mistaking for weakness the humanitarianism, the love of art, science, philosophy, and literature which make us hate the ravages of war. Yet now, because we must at all costs hold the temples of these ideals which have built up our civilization, we shall be the more empowered to fight. There is no greater moral force than the united armies of democracy.' The writer concluded with a spirited reference to one of Mr Churchill's broadcasts, which had recalled the story of the Maccabees, 'patriots who fought against the superior might of an alien tyranny with unconquerable resolve'.

War debates in the House of Commons were seen as 'an inspiring example of the democratic principle in action', and the paper supported the right of Englishmen to demand free discussion even in a time of national crisis such as the present. Democratic practice demanded political maturity and balance, and the task of the democratic leader was shown to be inevitably more difficult than that of his despotic opponent.

The war was a searching challenge for the British Commonwealth, bringing to this country a deep sense of the Empire's significance not only to ourselves but to the whole world. With Hong Kong, Malaya, and Burma in Japanese hands,

India threatened, and our kinsmen in Australia under the menace of imminent attack, *The Yorkshire Post* saw the issue as that of 'two rival conceptions of Empire' and declared: 'The British Empire stands for a great positive idea. It is in itself one of the main buttresses of the principles of law, freedom, and humanity throughout the world.' Urging the need to look beyond the present emergency it added:

But, if we are bound to think principally of the defence of the Commonwealth at this moment, it is good that we should think also of its future progress. It is evolving all the time as its component parts reach higher stages of political growth. The rate of this process depends not only upon the native races themselves, but also upon the effort which we, as a people, are prepared to put into the work of development.

In lighter vein, 'This World of Ours' continued to discuss topics of the day. It will present a rewarding source for the future historian in search of details about life in Britain during the war. 'What boots it to complain?' asked Northerner II during the leather shortage. 'If your boot repairer regrets that he cannot promise to sole and heel your shoes before the middle of next week, don't grumble, he may be refettling the footgear of the B.E.F.' In 1941 'This World' took great interest in a Wakefield reader's discovery of an old copy of *The Leeds Intelligencer* published in June 1813, during the Napoleonic Wars – noting that our forefathers were more fortunate than we in their 'Stilton, Wiltshire, Cheshire, Trentside, and Lancashire Cheeses' still 'sold at the lowest prices to dealers and housekeepers'. Candle rationing, shortage of diaries, the limited sale of fruit trees, and dwindling supplies of men's ties were among the privations wittily discussed by Northerner II; and his readers responded often in the same spirited mood.

A graphic picture of how *The Yorkshire Post* met war-time difficulties and news problems was given in a B.B.C. broadcast to the United States under the title 'Democracy Marches' in November 1941. William Holt gave listeners a vivid word picture of one of the paper's editorial conferences, held every evening at six o'clock, when the assistant editors, sub-editors, news editor and other chief men of the paper discussed the news and proposed subjects for the day's features with a view to their most effective presentation on the news page. He told also how they went on to discuss the best subjects for leading articles and special articles. Mr Holt added:

It wasn't at all like the newspaper editorial conferences you see in films. And yet the background was war, and there might have been a bombing raid that night. All was ready for it if it had come, and duplicate apparatus was prepared in the great cellars. No one could say what news might come over the wires during the night. Plans then being made might have to be scrapped at the last minute, but meanwhile all went on as the first steps were taken in the making of the next day's newspaper, the editor sharing his thoughts with his colleagues, suggesting a new line of inquiry here and there. It was all good team work.

Describing the journal's policy, Mr Holt said:

It's a Conservative paper based on a vast industrial population, it is a great commercial organ and it has also a strong appeal to farmers. It has been described as the most authoritative paper in the country in its discussions of Church of England policy. It has always been true to the best traditions of fair play, and like *The Manchester Guardian*, the great Liberal paper I talked to you about the other week, it has the courage to face unpopularity if something has had to be said that it feels ought to be said.

And his concluding thoughts were of a new function which *The Yorkshire Post* was now performing – the monthly compilation of blackout tables for the use of its readers. 'Every night', he said, 'these times move a few seconds as the nights draw in, and the times vary in different parts of Yorkshire. The readers cut out these tables and pin them up in their homes . . . Preparing blackout time-tables – that's a function your papers haven't need to perform yet.'

In the battle zones the paper was ably served during this period by Joe Illingworth. At the outset of the war he toured the bombed areas of England, and wrote many feature articles on the 'Blitz'. In 1943 he went to North Africa and to Italy as an air correspondent, and from D-day onwards was the paper's European war correspondent. In recognition of his services he was Mentioned in Dispatches. He remained in Germany until 1946, observing post-war conditions, and at the end of 1946 he visited the United States. Later he revisited Germany and wrote a series of valuable articles as a result of his investigations into industrial and domestic conditions in that country. He is now in Fleet Street as London editor of *The Yorkshire Post*. Many Yorkshire readers will remember Joe Illingworth's spirited accounts of how their sons were faring in Germany in 1945, when he accompanied the British Second Army as the 'eyes and ears' of this newspaper abroad. More recently he has visited the troops in Malaya. His efforts, and those of other members of the staff, have built up a strong tradition of care for the welfare of the Servicemen overseas to whom the paper and its representatives have come as friends and links with home.

In August 1944 appeared the famous *Kriegie* Edition of *The Yorkshire Post*. It was produced by members of the White Rose Club of Stalag Luft 6, East Prussia: *kriegie* being the German abbreviation for 'prisoner of war'. In the form of a large size magazine, it had plywood covers, stained to the colour of seasoned oak 'with brown shoe polish plus elbow grease', and joined with a spine of green linen. Deeply carved on the front cover was the title, *The Yorkshire Post* in its familiar Old English lettering, with the white rose of the county, on which was superimposed another strip of plywood bearing the carved inscription 'Kriegie Edition'. The editor was Richard B. Pape, who had been on the staff of the publicity department of the morning and evening papers

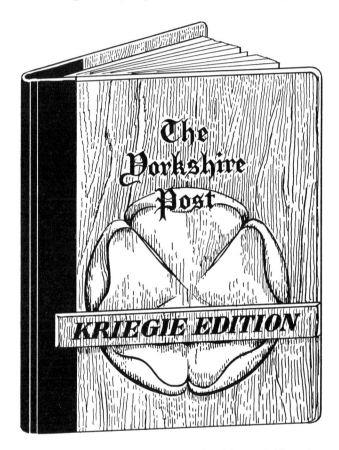

The 'Kriegie Edition' of The Yorkshire Post, *produced by Yorkshire prisoners in a German P.O.W. camp during the Second World War.*

until he joined the R.A.F. *The Yorkshire Post* prepared a souvenir edition of this brave venture and sent a copy to the families of the 254 members of the White Rose Club whose names appeared in the *Kriegie* Edition. Mr Churchill wrote of the souvenir booklet:

It is an interesting and moving record of the talent shown by these prisoners during the years of their captivity, and I am glad that *The Yorkshire Post* has decided to preserve their achievement by printing a reproduction of the work.

Among the many campaigns to maintain public morale at the period was the Exhibition of War Photographs organized by *The Yorkshire Post* in association with the *New York Times*. This was opened by Lieutenant-Commander Herbert Agar in November 1942. The Exhibition covered every phase of the great American arms drive, and its object was 'to make the two peoples understand their common war effort'. In the same year the paper organized a 'Russia at War' exhibition, which showed over 500 photographs giving many aspects of Russian life – in the services, the cities, the workshops, and the nurseries.

Both *The Yorkshire Post* and *The Leeds Mercury* have shown down the years a close interest in social questions and this tradition has been strongly maintained since they joined forces. Such topics as the care of old people, child welfare, family allowances, housing and slum clearance, the problem of juvenile delinquency, and prison reform have been dealt with thoroughly and sympathetically. The journal has not been content merely to report what has been said on these subjects or to comment on them in its leader columns. Again and again investigations have been conducted by senior members of the staff and new facts have been brought to light. In this way the paper has sought to draw attention to social needs, to influence public opinion, and to help in forming local and national policy.

When the tide of war began to turn and ideas for post-war reconstruction came up for discussion, *The Yorkshire Post* put its full weight behind the effort to draw up a programme of social reform upon which the main parties could agree. Its attitude was shown when the famous Beveridge report was published in December 1942. Giving the Beveridge plan its broad approval, the paper wrote:

A decision that its main features were to be carried into action as soon as possible after the war would make this country a pioneer of social reform in the world's eyes. Such a decision, moreover, would be a most heartening affirmation of faith in the future of Britain and in the constructive vitality of the democratic principle we are fighting to defend . . . The pioneering vision of the Beveridge report will quicken our war effort at home; it will encourage our friends abroad; it will refute the favourite jeering of our enemies about the effeteness of this ancient land. Through the boldness of his planning for peace Sir William Beveridge may well be numbered among the architects of victory.

But in all its discussion of this great project *The Yorkshire Post* stressed the essential point that the Beveridge proposals were a challenge to hard work. It warned the nation against comfortable notions that individual effort was no longer needed since the State would provide. It emphasized the vital importance of creating new national wealth to replace Britain's severe wartime losses. When the social security scheme was published in September 1944, the paper wrote: 'The aims of social planning must be not only to abolish poverty, but to foster the spirit of enterprise'. The justice of its comments, made on 26 September 1944, can be seen today. Saying that the scheme's aims were to end want and give every citizen the assurance of security in his old age, the paper added:

Can they be realized? The Government thinks that they can. It will try hard to achieve a great economic transformation, even though many think we shall have to contend in the next decade or so with world trade conditions that will make economic transformation a task of daunting difficulty. With the publication of this plan the Government has declared war upon poverty in our midst. This war will demand a unified national effort, such as has been shown in the war against Nazi Germany . . .

Seeing this, *The Yorkshire Post* did its utmost in the remaining months of the war to foster national unity. When in October 1944 the threat arose of a return to Party strife, it expressed a wish that the wartime Coalition could be preserved to put into effect the reforms already envisaged in the Government White Papers that had been issued during the past months:

The wide agreement upon this great programme of social advance is in itself an expression of national solidarity, the wholesome fruits of the sense of unity and comradeship which the war has brought into being. Let the nation remain united to work for this advance as it has worked for victory.

CHAPTER XI

Peace and its problems

[1945–1954]

The end of the war did not, alas, bring immediate relief from the problems of the newspaper world. In 1947 it was announced that *The Yorkshire Post* must suffer some reduction of size in order to conserve supplies of newsprint, and the paper was brought down on some days to a four-page issue. In January 1949 three six-page and three four-page papers were appearing weekly and in the following month the price was increased from one penny to three-halfpence. The following year saw further cuts in newsprint and in April 1952 it was found necessary to raise the price to twopence. Since that time the paper has fluctuated in size, aiming always at the goal of an eight-page issue as its very minimum.

By 1947 all members of the staff had returned from the Forces, with the exception of National Servicemen, and although newsprint restrictions continued to curtail the size of all newspapers, great efforts were made to give the paper new enterprise, variety, and liveliness. It was decided to improve and overhaul plant and in that year a notable advance was made by the installation of a telephoto transmitter in London with a receiver in Leeds. By this means many up-to-date pictures of vivid news interest were obtained. In 1948 new offices were opened in Bradford at Broadway House, Market Street.

While seeking to cater for the widening interests of readers in these post-war days and to improve news services and methods of presentation, *The Yorkshire Post* sought to uphold the old traditions that have given the great regional papers their importance in the life of the country. 'The Provincial Press', said the Company's chairman about this time, 'has long had a reputation for public spirit, balance, and accuracy. That is the reputation that our newspapers will strive to maintain.'

The General Election of 1950 provided a particularly severe testing time when curtailed space still created difficulties; but the paper was given special mention in a book, *The British General Election of 1950*, by H. G. Nicholas, published by Macmillan. In this the author said:

In England, perhaps the closest counterpart to the *Glasgow Herald* and *The Scotsman* as a paper with a wide and influential as well as high-quality coverage is *The Yorkshire Post*. No less than they, it acquitted itself creditably in its treatment of the election and cast its weight, similarly, into the Conservative side of the scales.

During the post-war period *The Yorkshire Post* continued to print its open and fearless comment on foreign affairs. In 1948 the paper's first leader asked 'Who is lying?' in its headline, and considered that 'there are times when it is an honour to be singled out for attack'. The occasion was the accusation levelled against *The Yorkshire Post*, among other British newspapers, by Dr A. Hoff-meister, the Czech ambassador-designate to France. Speaking at the Geneva Conference on the freedom of the Press, Dr Hoffmeister declared that these papers had 'deliberately lied' about what he described as the 'communistic victory in Czechoslovakia'. Pointing out that *The Yorkshire Post*'s efforts both during and after the war had been consistently directed towards the mainten-ance of friendship between the peoples of Russia and of Great Britain, the leader writer added with prophetic insight:

The lights are going out all over Europe. That is what Sir Edward Grey, the Foreign Secretary, said on the outbreak of war in 1914, and that, unhappily, is what we must reiterate today. Almost visibly the Iron Curtain is going down over Czechoslovakia.

For some time the paper's editorials and foreign correspondence had been closely watched by *Pravda*. In May 1945 M. Viktorov, writing in that journal, resented 'references in *The Yorkshire Post* to enigmatic aspects of Russian policy'. He added: '*The Yorkshire Post* calls the Russian policy a veritable riddle. Apparently it is the vogue to speak of Russia with the help of question marks.' The following year *Pravda* singled out *The Times* and *The Yorkshire Post* for criticism:

The Times is seconded by another Conservative British organ *The Yorkshire Post*. The only difference is that *The Times* suffers from a 'strange impression', while *The Yorkshire Post* in connexion with the Soviet representative's demand is stricken by 'gloomy foreboding'.

The Yorkshire Post reference was to a comment in an article printed in the paper on 25 April by M. R. Werner, its correspondent at the Conference of the United Nations Organization. Werner had said: 'There is a gloomy feeling in UNO circles that Soviet action in Persia portends her intention to defy the majority whenever she finds herself involved in a minority on questions in-volving her interests.'

In January 1950, a leading article spoke of derationing in the German

Federal Republic, and called attention to the privation and suffering which this might cause. Its statements were challenged by the *Daily Express*, but the paper maintained its viewpoint and replied to the *Express* by publishing a long and detailed report from its special correspondent in Bonn, reviewing the economic situation in Western Germany point by point. Another leading article reaffirmed the attitude already taken.

Tribute to the bold editorial policy of the paper in these critical years of reconstruction was paid by the weekly review *Truth*, which declared that 'the reputation of *The Yorkshire Post* during the past few years had grown far beyond its old bounds'. The writer said also that the journal had won 'a national reputation as the symbol of Yorkshire common sense and courage'. With transatlantic freshness, the American magazine *Newsweek* – the fierce competitor of *Time* – found a new description of *The Yorkshire Post* for the people of the United States. The paper was most aptly dubbed: 'The solidly conservative paterfamilias of England's wool production centre of Leeds', a title which certainly summed up happily an aspect of its history since the early days of *The Leeds Intelligencer*.

During the investigations of The Royal Commission on the Press in 1948, the company was represented by the Hon. Rupert Beckett, Mr Andrews and Mr Horniblow, of the *Evening Post*. The editor of *The Yorkshire Post* fought vigorously throughout this period both in the columns of the paper and in his public speeches for the maintenance of high traditions of editorial integrity. Noting his forthright comment, an American journal, the *Louisville Times,* said: 'Once again *Yorkshire Post* editor Mr W. L. Andrews speaks forcibly and to the point. He is a writer of strength and vigour, and a great figure in the British Press.' Lecturing in Yorkshire on 'A Free Press', in August 1949, Mr Andrews told his audience that the doctrine of the freedom of the Press, though long honoured in Britain, must not be regarded as secure. He felt that some of the old battles might have to be fought over again, if certain extremists attacking traditional methods of ownership and control had their way.

In March 1950 the Hon. Rupert E. Beckett retired, after thirty years of service as chairman and forty-four as a director of the Company. His was a distinguished record, and a sincere tribute was paid to him by his colleagues. 'He has always been beloved by all the staff', they said, 'and the name of Beckett will live as long as Leeds lasts'. Mr T. L. Taylor, who became a month later Mr Beckett's successor as chairman, said that at the time of Mr Beckett's appointment the Company was in a sound position, but he now left it in a very much improved and appreciably stronger position. He spoke also of the important decision which Mr Beckett had had to make concerning the amalgamation of *The Yorkshire Post* and *The Leeds Mercury*. This great venture was now vindicated by its success, and it had, indeed, 'proved of greater value to the Company than even the most optimistic had imagined'. Mr Beckett, in turn, spoke warmly of the support given to him as chairman by all the personnel of *The Yorkshire Post* and its allied papers, and declared: 'It would be foolish to deny that a chairman without the loyal support and the constant effort of those by whom he is surrounded could make but a poor job of such a brittle thing as a newspaper, depending as it does on an efficient management on the technical side, and a nice sense of news values, to make it popular without being sensational. That has been the ambition of all our editors.' He recalled that his father was the first chairman in 1866, holding office until 1890; and that his cousin, Lord Faber, then followed as chairman until 1920. Three years after Mr Beckett's retirement a portrait of him, a replica of one at the Westminster Bank's Leeds headquarters, took its place in the Company's boardroom, side by side with those of his father and his cousin. The artist was Mr Henry Carr, and the portrait was unveiled by Major Stanley Pearson.

In April 1950 the Board elected Mr T. L. Taylor as the new chairman. Mr Taylor had been a director for thirty years. He is widely known both as a leading figure in the engineering industry and as president of the Yorkshire County Cricket Club. His business career has been distinguished. He has been chairman and managing director of his family concern Taylor Brothers and Co., of Trafford Park, Manchester, and has served on the Board of management of Vickers Ltd. He has also been chairman of the Metropolitan Carriage, Wagon, and Finance Corporation, of Birmingham. This organization was formed under terms of agreement between Messrs Cammell Laird and Messrs Vickers for a fusion of stock interests, with an authorized share capital of more than £10,500,000. In his younger days Mr Taylor was a brilliant cricketer and all-round sportsman. He captained Cambridge, and did invaluable service as a resolute batsman for Yorkshire from 1899 to 1906 when he retired from the game for business reasons. He excelled also at hockey and at lawn tennis. He played hockey for Cambridge for four seasons, captaining the team in his last season; and at lawn tennis he won the Yorkshire doubles championship with Mr Sidney Watson in 1922 and 1923, and the mixed doubles title, playing with Miss Willans, in 1924.

The new vice-chairman of the Company was Mr Colin G. Forbes Adam, a man both of scholarly distinction and wide experience of affairs. Mr Forbes Adam was a member of the Indian Civil Service from 1912 to 1927. He served as private secretary to the Governor of Bombay from 1920 to 1925 and as deputy secretary to the Government during the last two years of his career in

The Board Room, which still bears traces of having been a room in a private house seventy years ago.
The large canvas is a portrait of the Hon. Rupert Beckett.

The room in which The Yorkshire Post *has been edited for seventy years. Over the mantelpiece are caricatures of Victorian states-*
men by Spy and Ape: in the fireplace is the copper kettle which J. S. R. Phillips used for tea making during the First World War.

The central office of the paper that has its heart in the North: Change Court, Albion Street, Leeds.

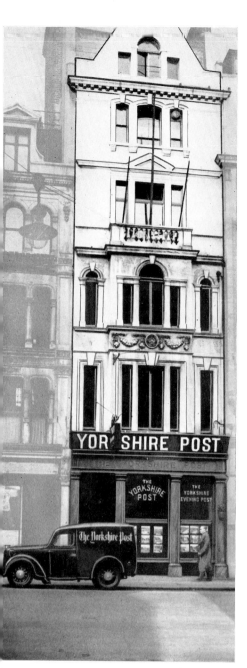

The Doncaster office.

The London office of The Yorkshire Post.

The Bradford office.

The case room of The Yorkshire Post *is one of the largest in the country. Here the type is set and the pages are assembled.*

The giant Crabtree rotary printing press in the machine room of The Yorkshire Post *can produce up to 160,000 twenty-page papers per hour.*

The Yorkshire Post *of 1954 is printed swiftly on electrically-driven rotary presses.*

India. Later from 1934 to 1939 he was district commissioner for the special area of Durham and Tyneside. He is the author of a biography of the first Lord Lloyd.

At the meeting at which Mr Taylor was elected chairman, Mr Ernest Osborn, the general manager, whose long and fruitful period of service with the Company dates back to 1901, was elected to the Board of directors. Mr Osborn has become a widely respected and influential personality in the newspaper world. An experienced member of the Newspaper Society, he was president of the Yorkshire Newspaper Society in 1942 and 1943. He is a past president and founder of the Leeds Publicity Club.

Mr Taylor announced to the shareholders in March 1953, that a pension scheme covering all employees between the ages of 20 and 60 for men and 30 and 55 for women had started in May, and of the eligible employees 92·68 per cent joined the scheme and were very well satisfied with it.

The great national event of these later years was the Coronation of Queen Elizabeth II on 2 June 1953. The following morning a twelve-page issue of *The Yorkshire Post* contained graphic reports of the ceremony in the Abbey, and of the great public rejoicings in London and the North. Inset on the leader page was the full text of the Queen's broadcast message to all her peoples on the evening of the Coronation. The first leader spoke of this message with deep sincerity:

With the Queen's candour and her warm, unaffected response to the nation's love and loyalty, goes a confidence that is wholly devoid of arrogance ... It springs from the profoundly religious sense which she displays. This sense Her Majesty may well help the nation to share. Imbued with it, the British peoples will command the power and conviction to do a notable service for all humanity, going forward together (in the Queen's own words) 'in peace, seeking justice and freedom for all men'. Can we, with the memory of yesterday's ceremony and the Queen's ardent faith to inspire us, give a torn and harassed world the lead it needs?

A second leader noted the wonder of the day in its 'Television Triumph'. *The Yorkshire Post* had consistently supported the televising of the ceremony in some of its stages, urging that 'it would be fitting to omit certain parts, but that the millions outside the Abbey ought to share in the rest'. Today its counsel stood vindicated by the unprecedented spectacle witnessed on television screens in millions of ordinary British homes. Signal enterprise was shown also on this occasion by *The Yorkshire Evening Post* which now, under the editorship of Mr. Alan Woodward, had a larger sale and more influence than ever before.

As the year drew to a close W. L. A. summed up its crises and its many fine records in his personal commentary 'It Seems to Me', a feature he had started in *The Leeds Mercury* thirty years previously. Writing in a spirit of quiet confidence, he recalled the treasured memory of the Coronation, and the remarkable coincidence that the event was synchronized with the year's peak of achievement, the triumph of the Everest expedition. He saw that great victory as symbolizing 'what we need most as a nation for the coming year – discipline, cooperation, perseverance', and concluded on a note of hope for 1954:

Next year may be better still if we settle our problems without wasteful strikes and if Sir Winston Churchill's noble efforts for a friendlier world meet with due reward.

For *The Yorkshire Post* the year 1954 is momentous as that of its bicentenary, a great landmark in a proud and unbroken record of two centuries of development. Going back through the heavy, closely printed files of the paper, decade after decade, the ardent investigator catches a spirit of adventure, for it is a quest of outstanding historical interest. In it he finds the past coming to light and events recorded as our forefathers saw them, with many uncertainties still unresolved.

The physical growth of Leeds alone during the period covered by this chronicle has been remarkable. When the *Intelligencer* was born the city's population was 16,000; it is now over half a million. And in the same period the West Riding has become one of Britain's most populous regions.

The history of *The Yorkshire Post* through two centuries is inevitably a history of that populous, bustling, energetic region in which it has circulated for so long: and its character is the character of the North. It enjoys an international reputation but is Yorkshire to the backbone. It has every reason to face its third century with pride and confidence. It welcomes the future with the steady salute of a veteran.

APPENDIX

DIRECTORS OF

THE YORKSHIRE CONSERVATIVE NEWSPAPER COMPANY LIMITED

In the Company's articles of association, dated 8 February 1866, and effective from March, it was laid down: 'There shall be sixteen directors, each of whom shall hold not less than twenty shares in the Company.

'The first directors shall be:

Viscount Nevill
The Hon. George Lascelles
Francis Darwin
William Beckett Denison
Thomas Townend Dibb
John Ellershaw
Alfred Harris
Robert John Hudson

William Scarborough Jackson
William Thomas Jackson
John Towlerton Leather
John Pepper
John Robinson
John Musgrave Sagar-Musgrave
George Taylor
Robert Tennant'

The first meeting of the directors after the publication of *The Yorkshire Post and Leeds Intelligencer* took place on 6 July 1866. The following were present at the meeting:

W. Beckett Denison, *chairman*
Francis Darwin
R. J. Hudson
W. T. Jackson

John Ellershaw
J. M. Sagar-Musgrave
Robert Tennant
Thomas Townend Dibb

The minute books show that later directors were elected, or their first attendances at meetings recorded, on the dates given:

10 May 1867   Christopher Kemplay
                 William Middleton
2 April 1869   Edward Bond
11 February 1870   The Earl of Abergavenny (formerly Viscount Nevill) recommended for re-election to the Board
8 October 1870   John Taylor
28 March 1871   Joseph Holt
7 March 1873   John Ralph

13 August 1875	Lord Feversham
8 December 1876	H. Y. Nelson
2 July 1880	Gerard Lascelles Darwin
11 March 1881	W. L. Jackson, M.P.
	E. B. Faber (later Lord Faber)
21 March 1882	Darcy Bruce Wilson
20 March 1883	Sir H. B. Edwards
7 November 1883	William Middleton
19 September 1884	Colonel Gunter
2 April 1886	John Thomas Pearson

In 1887 it was decided that the number of directors should gradually be
reduced to nine and that any director who failed to attend a meeting for six
consecutive months should automatically cease to be a member of the Board.
By the application of this resolution the number of directors had been reduced
to nine by 9 April 1888, and the Board then consisted of:

William Beckett, *chairman*	Darcy Bruce Wilson
John Ellershaw	The Hon. George E. Lascelles
E. B. Faber	Francis Darwin
John Musgrave Sagar-Musgrave	J. T. Pearson
William Middleton	

The following dates are of minute-book references to the appointment,
resignations or deaths of directors:

8 September 1890	John Ellershaw resigned
30 September 1890	Richard Hale Braithwaite appointed
2 December 1890	Death of William Beckett
	Appointment of Edmund Beckett Faber (later Lord Faber) as chairman
16 December 1890	Ernest William Beckett (later Lord Grimthorpe) appointed
20 February 1893	Arthur Tredgold Lawson appointed: elected vice-chairman on 30 October 1894
13 March 1894	The Hon. George E. Lascelles resigned
24 April 1894	William Gervase Beckett appointed
19 April 1904	William Middleton died
20 September 1904	J. T. Pearson died
	Marshall Nicholson appointed
10 October 1904	Francis Stanley Jackson appointed
16 May 1905	R. H. Braithwaite died
1 August 1905	Lord Grimthorpe resigned

1 May 1906	J. M. Sagar-Musgrave died
8 May 1906	The Hon. Rupert Evelyn Beckett, Abraham Musgrave, Sagar-Musgrave, and William Henry Maude appointed
22 August 1911	W. H. Maude died
5 June 1915	Sir Arthur Lawson died
	The Hon. Rupert Beckett appointed vice-chairman
4 January 1916	Marshall Nicholson died
11 January 1916	Major Robert Stanley Pearson appointed
25 January 1916	Francis Alvey Darwin appointed
27 January 1920	Lord Faber resigned chairmanship
	The Hon. Rupert Beckett elected chairman
September 1920	Lord Faber died
18 March 1921	Tom Lancelot Taylor appointed
14 December 1923	Sir John Eaglesome appointed (resigned May 1946)
10 July 1931	Albany Kenneth Charlesworth appointed (killed on active service, February 1945)
13 May 1938	Colin Gurdon Forbes Adam appointed
22 September 1939	Col. Hugh Delabere Bousfield appointed (died July 1951)
28 March 1941	A. M. Sagar-Musgrave resigned
18 April 1941	Cecil Lawies Sagar-Musgrave appointed
23 February 1945	Commander Jameson Boyd Adams appointed (resigned January 1950)
12 September 1946	Brigadier Arthur Maxwell Ramsden appointed
15 August, 1947	The Hon. Richard Frederick Wood appointed
18 November 1949	W. L. Andrews appointed
14 April 1950	The Hon. Rupert Beckett resigned
	T. L. Taylor elected chairman
	Ernest Osborn appointed
4 January 1952	Kenneth Wade Parkinson appointed

Present Members of the Board

Tom Lancelot Taylor, *chairman*
Colin Gurdon Forbes Adam, c.s.i., *vice-chairman*
Cecil Lawies Sagar-Musgrave, m.c.
Brigadier Sir Arthur Maxwell Ramsden, c.b., o.b.e., t.d., d.l.
The Hon. Richard Frederick Wood, m.p.
William Linton Andrews
Ernest Osborn
Kenneth Wade Parkinson

INDEX